The Elusive Self *in the* Poetry *of*

ROBERT BROWNING

The
Elusive Self
in the Poetry of
ROBERT

BROWNING

by Constance W. Hassett

OHIO UNIVERSITY PRESS
ATHENS, OHIO

Library of Congress Cataloging in Publication Data

Hassett, Constance W., 1943–
    The elusive self in the poetry of Robert Browning.

    Includes bibliographical references and index.
    1. Browning, Robert, 1812–1889—Criticism and inter-
pretation. 2. Self in literature. I. Title.
PR4242.S46H37   1982   821'.8   81-22575
ISBN 0-8214-0629-9   AACR2

Contents

Acknowledgments

I am pleased to express thanks to Jerome H. Buckley. He once asked, in the most disarming fashion, "Do you have any ideas about Browning?" and committed himself generously to helping me develop my answer to his question. I am grateful as well to John Maynard. His suggestions at crucial stages were invaluable; no anxiety of mine ever drained his enthusiasm and no demand on his time was too outrageous. I am also in the debt of Thomas J. Collins who painstakingly read and commented on the manuscript. The book would not have taken its present form without his helpful recommendation on how to extend its scope. Thanks are due also to the American Council of Learned Societies and to the Fordham University Research Council for grants that aided in the preparation of the book and to the editor of *Philological Quarterly* for permission to use an article that first appeared there, "Browning's Caponsacchi: Convert and Apocalyptist." I must thank, too, the people connected with Ohio University Press: Allan Dooley for his candor and generosity as a reader, Lurene Brown for her tactfulness as a copy editor, and Helen Gawthrop for her efficient assistance in many areas.

Finally I am happy to indicate a very special indebtedness to James Richardson. Our discovery that we held similar views of Browning led to many conversations that have seriously influenced my thought. To him and to our daughter Connie this book is dedicated.

1

"In the Confessing Vein"

Browning's first published work was issued anonymously, read only by reviewers, and deliberately neglected by the poet himself. Fourteen years later, however, Dante Gabriel Rossetti found a copy of *Pauline: A Fragment of a Confession* in the British Museum and correctly guessed its author.[1] Rossetti's acuity is compelling, for it raises the issue of Browning's distinctiveness and leads to consideration of the traits and preoccupations that are uniquely his own. Readers who think of Browning as the master of the grotesque, the creator of outrageous characters such as Porphyria's crazed admirer, are not likely, at first glance, to recognize Pauline's lover as one of his speakers. A vaguely drawn young poet, he talks at length of his aspirations and disillusionments. And to readers who expect all Browning's poems to sound more or less like "The Soliloquy of the Spanish Cloister," to those who regard Browning's style as energetically clotted, the smoothly melancholy blank verse of *Pauline* does not sound familiar:

> Thou wilt remember one warm morn. . .
> . . . .
> I walked with thee who knew'st not a deep shame
> Lurked beneath smiles and careless words which sought
> To hide it till they wandered and were mute,

> As we stood listening on a sunny mound
> To the wind murmuring in the damp copse,
> Like heavy breathings of some hidden thing
> Betrayed by sleep; until the feeling rushed
> That I was low indeed, yet not so low
> As to endure the calmness of thine eyes.
> And so I told thee all, while the cool breast
> I leaned on altered not its quiet beating:
> And long ere words like a hurt bird's complaint
> Bade me look up and be what I had been,
> I felt despair could never live by thee.   (ll. 55, 62–75).[2]

Yet this passage is typical in its context of much of Browning's poetry, for here the speaker remembers and resumes the one activity that fascinates Browning throughout his career: Pauline's lover has told and will again tell his lady "all." He speaks "in the confessing vein" (*Paracelsus*, III.664) that characterizes not only Browning's early narratives but his mature monologues, *The Ring and the Book*, and some of the later works as well. *Pauline: A Fragment of a Confession* is the first of many poems in which an individual surveys his life and considers his deficiencies. The Bishop of St. Praxed's has "strange thoughts" (l. 91)

> About the life before I lived this life,
> And this life, too, popes, cardinals and priests.
> . . . .
> Evil and brief hath been my pilgrimage.   (ll. 93–94, 101).

Fra Lippo Lippi offers an account of his boyhood to explain away his sensuality:

> Well, well, there's my life in short,
> And so the thing has gone on ever since.
> I'm grown a man no doubt, I've broken bounds:
> You should not take a fellow eight years old
> And make him swear to never kiss the girls.   (ll. 221–25).

The defiant medium Mr. Sludge recalls his apprenticeship and "vomits" up some nasty truths:

> You've heard what I confess; I don't unsay
> A single word: I cheated when I could.   (ll. 799–800).

In *The Ring and the Book*, Caponsacchi reassesses his entire life and priesthood:

> I was born, have lived, shall die, a fool!
> . . . .
> . . . But, all the same, I know
> I too am taintless, and I bare my breast.   (VI. 181, 196–97).

And Hohenstiel-Schwangau imagines a double "revealment" (I. 22) of himself: the first installment,

> All . . . to my praise and glory—all
> Told as befits the self-apologist,—   (ll. 1202–03),

complemented by a second:

> Autobiography, adieu! The rest
> Shall make amends, be pure blame, history
> And falsehood.   (ll. 1220–21).

The motive behind such soul-baring, the urgent but often compromised impulse to determine one's worth, is the fundamental issue in Browning's art. Fascinated with man's energy for self-assessment, he makes the problem of honest scrutiny his dominant concern. The confessional mode, as used by his speakers, is more than a simple excursion into the past. Retrospection is a form of introspection; and memory, a technique for self-confrontation. The process of autobiography can, in Browning's view, alter a man's perception and supply the impetus for spiritual change. By bringing an individual to new terms with his identity, confession can facilitate the process of moral transformation. Such introspection, if genuine, is tantamount to a conversion.

Browning is hardly the first to be interested in man's need for self-knowledge or the turning points in its pursuit. These are the perennial issues of religious and secular autobiography. The reader of Augustine, Rousseau, Wesley, Wordsworth and a host of Victorian writers is familiar with the connection Browning posits between self-assessment and moral change. Browning's notion of "Action in Character"[3] is part of his Christian-European heritage. In *Natural Supernaturalism*, Meyer Abrams definitively treats the relation between Romantic psycho-biography and the writings of Paul and Augustine; and in *The Confessional Imagination*, Frank McConnell discusses the "shared concerns" of Wordsworth and the justified sinners of the dissenting persuasion.[4] The intention here is not to demonstrate Browning's indebtedness to a particular forebear, but to offer analogies that clarify Browning's poetic enterprise. The variety of works recognized as confessional is, of course, enormous, while the diversity of the experiences described as conversions is only slightly less remarkable. Though this richness poses problems for historians of genre, it is an advantage to the student of Browning. For within the limits of these almost undefinably broad and yet practically recognizable categories, the majority of Browning's poetry can be located.[5] When the legitimate variety of antecedent and contemporary forms is invoked, the much-ignored coherence of Browning's work becomes apparent. The affinity, for example, between poems as different as *Sordello* and *Pippa Passes* or "Bishop Blougram's Apology" and "Saul" becomes demonstrable. Nor is the unity that thus emerges a matter of huddling Browning's works under a large umbrella. The umbrella is welcome, to be sure, but the real advantage of referring Browning's poetry to the confessional tradition is that it clarifies his fundamental concerns at the same time that it directs attention to his vast originality. The similarities between the crises of many of his poems and those of the Christian confessants or the Romantic and Victorian autobiographers make plain how variously, yet how persistently, he imagines his characters in the process of transformation. For Browning, man is typically a convert.

The value of this recognition is that it illuminates individual poems—among them "The Flight of the Duchess" and Caponsacchi's monologue—while it leads to the further realization that some of Browning's greatest poems revolve obsessively around conversions that do *not* occur. Browning knows full well that self-confrontation can be painful, is a thing to be resisted, and that the past can be manipulated to make the present seem inevitable, right, or even best. He comprehends the difference between authentic and distorted confession. This distinction, moreover, is so basic to Browning's psychology that it leads him to develop—for Andrea del Sarto, Mr. Sludge, and others—a distinctive new genre, that of the confession manqué. For the present, a few brief comparisons will establish how diversely habitual is Browning's interest in conversions.

In *Pippa Passes*, he envisions a pair of murderous lovers at the very moment of their shared moral awakening. The event has the drama and suddenness of a Methodist convert's conviction of sin. Moved to repent by a confrontation with innocence, Sebald and Ottima undergo "justification" as conspicuous as any "outward change . . . from drunkenness to sobriety, from robbery or theft to honesty" reported among John Wesley's auditors.[6] The episode begins recollectively as the exultant Ottima savors the memory of her first adultery with Sebald. She imagines herself "magnificent in sin" (I. 218), perversely worthy of divine attention, yet thrillingly beyond the reach of God's punishing messenger:

> Buried in the woods we lay, you recollect;
> Swift ran the searching tempest overhead;
> And ever and anon some bright white shaft
> Burned thro' the pine-tree roof, here burned and there,
> As if God's messenger thro' the close wood screen
> Plunged and replunged his weapon at a venture
> Feeling for guilty thee and me.   (I. 190–96).

Intervention occurs, but not in the form of crudely intrusive thunderbolts. God's agent is the lowly Pippa. Her song so moves Sebald that he abandons his delusion that "guilt from its excess [is] superior / To innocence" (I. 260–61). His sudden, anguished, and radical change compels Ottima's repentance as well. Browning's concern in this short drama is not whether the lovers become assured of divine forgiveness; indeed, since they end in double suicide, some readers have doubted their salvation. His interest is the form of the event and the psychology of the lovers' conversion.[7] They are not stricken with simple feelings of wrongdoing; they are afflicted with a fundamental and terrible self-loathing. As Browning conceives of it, revulsion from error is not the reappraisal of some external ethos; it involves the rejection of what is evil or inauthentic in one's own identity. The essence of conversion is self-confrontation. In Sebald's case, the recognition of sin is represented as a form of self-alienation, and Browning dwells vividly on its turbulence. Ominous images suggest the rush of disintegration and the chaos of transformation:

> all I feel
> Is . . . is, at swift-recurring intervals,
> A hurry-down within me, as of waters
> Loosened to smother up some ghastly pit:
> There they go—whirls from a black fiery sea!   (I. 277–81).

This deep confusion is the necessary consequence of relinquishing his sinner's identity. He feels the terror of passage, the same terror that Saul, Roland and Caponsacchi feel each in his turn.

The fear of such dissolution causes some of Browning's characters to balk at conversion. They seem to know transforming truths and yet they cling to their identities. Sordello resorts to sophistries in order to delay commitment, Karshish defers setting his thoughts in order rather than succumb to the influence of Lazarus, and even the speaker of "By the Fire-side" hesitates to declare his love. For others, the dread of such unselving is more primal, subverting self-scrutiny and preventing the discoveries that jeopardize their identities. Andrea del Sarto, the "Pictor Ignotus," and the Bishop of St. Praxed's are among these; they review their lives without ever recognizing their souls' deficiencies. Browning is intrigued by the obstacles that make potential converts falter and by the whole problem of psychological resistance. Whether he conceives of a character as refusing or finally yielding to the forces of renovation, his most provocative poems acknowledge the *difficulties* of such change. Again and again, he stresses the tension between man's competing instincts for psychic renewal and self-preservation.

Conversions in Browning's poetry are not ordinarily so lurid as in *Pippa Passes*. In general, his successful converts bear a stronger family resemblance to the dejected hero of *Pauline* than to the depraved Ottima and Sebald. Not surprisingly, they also bear a likeness to Browning himself who, from the distance of middle age, recalls for Julia Wedgwood his own early hopelessness; "[D]o you know, a phrenologist told me when I was about sixteen that I had absolutely no hope at all in the head of me—and so it really was in those days."[8] Like their author, Browning's characters need to be saved less from passionate sensuality than from aimlessness and emotional aridity. In this respect Browning follows the strand of evangelical tradition that stresses the awakened sinner's spiritual desolation and the effect of newly apprehended guilt. Religious conversion, in this context, is represented as the transition from despair of salvation to trust in justification through Christ.[9] To put the matter another way, a full conversion is a two-fold experience. It begins with the recognition of one's waywardness—often prompted by a sermon—but ends with a more subtle crisis—like Wesley's own "Aldersgate experience"—that leaves one assured of salvation.[10] Although these are often collapsed into one, they are nonetheless distinguishable episodes. Both accomplish significant interior change, but of radically different kinds. The first is characterized by violent remorse whereas the second involves the passage from anxiety to peace. The one is primarily a matter of self-recrimination; the other, because it alleviates spiritual doubt, a joyful and positive experience. It is this latter change that is relevant to *Pauline*. Although this poem is certainly not Methodist nor even specifically evangelical, it does concern a change in the speaker's relationship with God as he passes from atheism to belief. More noteworthy still is the way this spiritual renewal is paralleled by the resolution of the speaker's aesthetic and political crises. The consequence of such reduplication is a very flexible conversion pattern, one that retains the seriousness while modifying the content of the strictly religious model.

The threads of conversion necessarily intertwine in *Pauline* but can be discerned with little difficulty. A Christian who no longer believes in God, the speaker is also a disappointed Promethean. Possessed of an ardent nature and fired by chiliastic dreams, he was once "vowed to Liberty, / Men were to be as gods and earth as heaven" (ll. 425-26). The failure to realize these goals has plunged him into a state of total disillusionment:

> First went my hopes of perfecting mankind,
> Next—faith in them, and then in freedom's self
> And virtue's self, then my own motives, ends
> And aims and loves, and human love went last.   (ll. 458-61).

A devastating torpor now undermines all human relationships, causing him, in his loveless isolation, to resemble the hero of Shelley's "Alastor"—one of those who "keep aloof from sympathies with their kind"[11]—and the young John Stuart Mill. The disenchanted dreamer is also a failed poet. This third aspect of the poem has received more attention than any other since it reveals the history of Browning's aesthetic relationship with Shelley. In his comprehensive discussion in *Browning's Youth*, John Maynard describes Browning's response to the Sun-treader as a "poetic conversion" that might well have "overshadowed and destroyed Browning's own different propensities" as poet.[12] The undermining of this conversion and the consequences thereof are recorded in *Pauline*:

> [T]he ultimate integration of the insights he had gained from Shelley into his mature poetic work was . . . a thing of the distant future. At the time, he was left with quite a desperate situation. His identification with Shelley had focused most of his energies on assuming the role of poet. His initial and decisive swerve away from Shelley in [*Pauline*] left him with virtually nowhere to go.[13]

It takes Browning at least until the completion of *Sordello* to reconceive fully his poetic role. But in *Pauline*, the "desperate situation" is immediately remedied for Pauline's poet, if not for Browning himself, by the recovery of poetic aims. Frustrated in his efforts to mediate his visions, he has fallen willingly into a condition of imaginative solipsism. Like the unknown painter, like Andrea del Sarto, Aprile, and even Waring, the artist who cannot create takes the dubious course of hoarding his talent:

> 　　I ne'er may tell
> Half the bright sights which dazzle me; but now
> Mine shall be all the radiance: let them fade
> Untold.　　　　　　　　　　　　　　　(ll. 518–21).

Depleted by this triple defection and guilty about having "flung away / [His] youth's chief aims" (ll. 589–90), he endures the torment of spiritual barrenness and intense self-loathing:

> But I begin to know what thing hate is—
> To sicken and to quiver and grow white—
> And I myself have furnished its first prey.　　(ll. 650–52).

The ideals he can neither achieve nor guiltlessly relinquish end in dejection. Herein lies the opportunity Browning seizes to secularize the conversion pattern. He conceives of the plight of the individual who has lost his humanitarian and aesthetic confidence as essentially similar to that of the convicted sinner. A man's passage towards hope, whether his concerns are sacred or profane, is based on the reassessment of his being; and whatever the specific circumstances, the self is very much at stake.

This is not to suggest that *Pauline* is consciously modeled on some particular conversion narrative. Browning's use of the conversion pattern need not be attributed to any more specific source than the evangelical atmosphere in which he was raised. There is no evidence that any of the Brownings underwent emotional religious conversions; but, as John Maynard asserts,

> Emphasis in his family's religion would have been placed upon the periodic need to renew and advance the inner religious life . . . they certainly looked upon the religious life as primarily a matter of attaining to moments of heightened awareness and emotional conviction, to those times when . . . consciousness of God's goodness "melts the heart of those in Covenant with God" and the man is raised closer to his ultimate spiritual perfection.[14]

It is not hard to see how the idea of such "moments" could bear fruit in the many occasions of elevation, passage, and conversion scattered throughout Browning's work. Maynard adds further that "in this enterprise" of seeking heightened awareness, "special importance was given to the business of self-examination."[15] He finds, in short, a convincing link between the introspective nature of the Browning family's religion and the self-scrutinizing mode adopted by so many of Browning's speakers. These connections are borne out by the conclusion of *Pauline* where, after all his soul searching, the poet announces his threefold recovery and is lifted into a new and unnameable mood of faith, altruism, and aesthetic aspiration. His confession leads to his final avowal, "Sun-treader, I believe in God and truth / And love" (ll. 1020–21); and while he exhibits neither the humble nor the exultingly confident varieties of certitude, the speaker believes himself a convert.

This assessment seems to have been shared by Browning's friend

Alfred Domett. He remarks in a letter that *Pauline* concerns Browning's "own early life as it presented itself to his own soul viewed poetically."[16] Despite this teasingly biographical beginning, Domett resists the temptation to gossip about the young poet and comments instead on the similarity of the poem, "psychologically speaking," to Carlyle's *Sartor Resartus*. In effect, Domett places *Pauline* within the literary genre Jerome Buckley describes in his seminal chapter on "The Pattern of Conversion" in Victorian literature. Buckley points out that the notion of conversion or "the soul's rebirth to 'higher things' " animates "the whole gospel of *Sartor Resartus*,"[17] and this is surely what Domett had in mind when he compared the two. Domett could, moreover, have included a string of contemporary titles; for as Buckley makes clear, conversions of one kind or another characterize the Victorian experience. The conversion genre was so omnipresent culturally that Browning could hardly have remained impervious. There are so many self-scrutinizing nineteenth century works, bearing witness to so many spiritual renewals, that even if nothing were known of Browning's religious upbringing, his extensive use of "the confessing vein" could be accounted for by analogy with his contemporaries.

The dejection of Mill's *Autobiography*, for example, is very much like that of *Pauline*. In 1826 Mill asked himself an awful millenarian question and became profoundly depressed by the answer:

> "Suppose that all your objects in life were realized; that all the changes in institutions and opinions which you are looking forward to, could be completely effected at this very instant: would this be a great joy and happiness to you?" And an irrepressible self-consciousness distinctly answered, "No!" At this my heart sank within me: the whole foundation on which my life was constructed fell down. All my happiness was to have been found in the continual pursuit of this end. The end had ceased to charm. . . .[18]

Awakened from his utilitarian dream, Mill found that his own "interesting and animated existence" was dull, flat, and stale and that his "love of mankind . . . had worn itself out."[19] Though Pauline's hero is not so much worried about the quality of his own happiness as he is in despair of finding a goal he can wholeheartedly serve, his general disillusionment resembles Mill's. It also recalls the isolation and "spiritual destitutions" of Carlyle's Teufelsdröckh.[20] Unable to obey the precept "Know thyself" or "Know what thou canst work at," he castigates himself as "the completest Dullard of these modern times."[21] Wordworth's disillusionment in Book XI of *The Prelude*— even though unpublished until 1850—is relevant here, too. For as Robert Langbaum points out,

> Teufelsdröckh's period of emotional sterility has its parallel in Wordworth's career at the point when he too arrives at the dead-end of the eighteenth century—when, having lost faith in the French Revolution and having lost through over-use of the analytic "knife" the ability to believe in anything and therefore to feel and live, he "Yielded up," as he tells us in *The Prelude*, "moral questions in despair." "This," he says referring to the eighteenth-century disease of analysis,
>
> > was the crisis of that strong disease,
> > This the soul's last and lowest ebb.   (XI. 305–07).[22]

There is, in fact, no shortage of comparisons, for the late eighteenth and the nineteenth centuries are strewn with depressed and temporarily alienated personalities. Nor is there any difficulty relating their grimly anxious moods to that of religious desolation. It is noteworthy, however, that the secular Mill explicitly recognizes the affinity between his condition and that of the traditional convert. He admits the similarity between ethical and religious dejection; the discovery that he is bereft of a goal in life is as crushing as the religious man's fear of missing salvation. Mill is very specific in this matter and compares his state of hopelessness to that "in which converts to Methodism usually are, when smitten with their first 'conviction of sin.' " Both find that "what is pleasure at other times, becomes insipid or indifferent."[23]

This enervated condition is a leitmotif of Browning's poetry and serves to link otherwise very different characters. The once-vibrant wife in "The Flight of the Duchess" is so worn by imposed trivialities that she looks at her husband "as if pressed by fatigue even he could not dissipate" (ll. 284–85). She has an unlikely counterpart in the patriot of "The Italian in England." Oppressed by others' defections from the cause, he feels tired and dispirited; "Ah, there, what should I wish? For fast / Do I grow old and out of strength" (ll. 128–29).

Perhaps the weariest of all is Childe Roland who welcomes the prospect of failure and death,

>   neither pride
> Nor hope rekindling at the end descried,
>   So much as gladness that some end might be.   (ll. 16–18).

Such depletion is regarded by Browning as a stage in the saving process. Far from being a proof of spiritual destitution, such exhaustion is almost a predisposition for conversion. These characters suffer what Buckley, citing R. H. Hutton, describes as a salutary despair:

> for conversion, according to an able Anglican apologist, came not to the careless profligate, but rather to the troubled soul beset with a liberating "despair," a genuine weariness of the ego, and "a passionate desire to find some new centre of life" which might "renovate the springs and purify the aims of the soiled and exhausted nature."[24]

Browning's attitude towards such "liberating" desolation emerges clearly in the early *Paracelsus*. The sixteenth century mage has a unique position among Browning's heroes, for his career describes a repeating pattern of aspiration, "strangling failure," (I. 502) and restoration. His goal in life is

>   to comprehend the works of God,
> And God himself, and all God's intercourse
> With the human mind   (I. 533–35);

and he accepts religious truths only as earned and not as received tenets of belief. His effort to validate Christianity without benefit of tradition made him particularly appealing to nineteenth century readers, but the lasting significance of the poem lies less in the content of Paracelsus' achieved faith than in his recurring moods of dejection and the way they are transformed. Having dedicated himself to the pursuit of total knowledge, Paracelsus inevitably fails and is forced, at several stages of his career, to measure his "previous life's attainment" (II. 21) and to reassess his aims. His first retrospection is prompted, after a decade of labor, by the discovery that his once radiant sense of purpose has dimmed. As despondent as Coleridge's Ancient Mariner, he sickens, metaphorically, "on a dead gulf streaked with light / From its own putrefying depths alone" (II. 175–76). While in this demoralized condition, Paracelsus comes under the influence of Aprile, a poet who teaches him the importance of love, and eventually casts off despair. What is important in their encounter is the relationship between Paracelsus' bewilderment and his responsiveness. The vigorous pursuit of his life's one aim has, until now, made him impervious to others. His dedication to knowledge has been so arrogantly solitary that he has refused all advice that might have prevented his failure. Under these circumstances, exhaustion of spirit has unexpectedly fortunate consequences. Because he is too weary to defend his identity, his self-preserving instincts are in abeyance. He is, like Browning's other fatigued characters, so utterly depleted as to be unguarded, unresisting, and susceptible to influence. Paracelsus' passivity is not simply inertia, but a form of openness. After great exertion and expense of self, conversion is possible.

Despite Paracelsus' sense of fulfillment at the end of this episode, his renewal is only temporary. Launched on a career of partial attainments and successive depressions, he is less a convert than a lifelong convert-in-the-making. Throughout his entire career, he feels the alternating possibilities of vehement self-assertion and confessional reassessment; and his final restoration comes only with the approach of death. A feeble, embittered old man, he regards his life as irretrievably wasted, "spent and decided" (II. 40). An insight into the order of history prompts him, however, to survey his past one more time. He now makes consistent sense of what he had formerly supposed to be his faulty relationship with the world. Dejection is banished as his life's worth is finally and legitimately established. This change consummates the poem and embodies Browning's belief that irrevocable deeds are not fixed in value. Confession can shed the light of "new knowledge upon old events" (V. 507). The remembered past, the past that lives in the present, can be redeemed; or, to put the matter another way, the lived identity can be reclaimed.

Browning's early converts, particularly Sebald, Pauline's poet, and Paracelsus, have much in common. Their moods of shame, dejection and triumph suggest the varieties of self-esteem; each confronts himself and is changed by what he sees. Whether led to denounce his current role or re-embrace forsaken ideals, he is motivated by the act of revision. Browning's sense of the individual's private history involves more than the issue of self-esteem, however. He can conceive of situations that require fusion instead of renewal, conversions that resolve an individual's self-division. In *Pippa Passes*, for example, Luigi faces a crisis of will rather than of vision. The revolutionary young man hates tyranny and plans a desperate venture requiring the commitment of his whole being; "For the world's sake" (III. 53), he will assassinate the Austrian oppressor. Conceiving of political murder as a form of self-martyrdom, he longs to make a sacrifice for mankind. The dubiousness of the ethics should not distract the reader, for the point of the story is the testing of Luigi's commitment. A series of teachers have inspired his nationalism; and although he is a poor apologist for his cause, he is thoroughly convinced of its rightness:

> I understand
> But can't restate the matter; that's my boast:
> Others could reason it out to you, and prove
> Things they have made me feel.   (III. 142–45).

But despite his zeal, the would-be martyr is tempted to inaction, and the entire episode implies the difficulty of marshalling one's resources. The young man is sure of his cause but he is not now moved by it. The distinction subtly invokes two different conceptions of personality. There is the sense that one's identity is the product of gradual and natural process, that certitude is the work of time, as well as the opposite sense that identity is formed by crisis, that conversion is the work of the moment.

These are, of course, the two themes operative in confessional literature from Augustine onward; and the saint's experience as recorded in the *Confessions* is relevant to an understanding of Browning's purposes in Luigi's episode. Augustine's attainment of religious conviction, the gradual dispelling of philosophical doubt "concerning the incorruptible Substance" of the divine nature, was not sufficient to make him a convert (VIII.1). "The way itself, the Saviour, was pleasing, yet there was still some repugnance to walking His difficult ways" (VIII.1).[25] Augustine's eighth chapter describes the memorable choice of Christ's way and the sudden conversion of the saint's will. In Browning's poem, Luigi experiences a similar discontinuity between comprehending and willing. For him, as for Augustine, the galvanizing of the will is a discrete event, very different in nature from the gradual attainment of intellectual certainty. It takes an unexpected and apparently extraneous sign to move him to commitment; Pippa's song, like the cry of the Milanese child outside Augustine's garden, rouses the auditor's will. Both the song and the cry are sudden but efficacious, incidental but significant and motivating. Each enables its hearer to negotiate the distance between understanding and willed decision. This dual process of reorientation finds its fullest treatment in Browning in *The Ring and the Book*. Motivated by Pompilia, the priest Caponsacchi undergoes a distinctly twofold transformation. In recognizing her goodness he discovers his own but must endure a dark night of the soul before he acts the true priest's role.

Browning loves crisis and is imaginatively excited by decisive events. The momentous and the momentary are so often linked in his work that a personal myth seems likely. He rarely conceives of the movement from dejection to hope, from error to truth, or from simple comprehension to activated understanding as a smooth progression. Self-apprehension occurs by fits and starts and is most often represented by what Meyer Abrams calls a "right-angled" event. Abrams uses this phrase to describe the pattern of Biblical history:

> While the main line of change in the prominent classical patterns of history, whether primitivist or cyclical, is continuous and gradual, the line of change in Christian history (and this difference is pregnant with consequences) is right-angled: the key events are abrupt, cataclysmic, and make a drastic, even absolute, difference. Suddenly, out of nothing, the world is created by divine fiat. There is a precipitous fall from a deathless felicity into a mortal life of corruption and anguish in a stricken world. The birth of the Redeemer, at a precise instant in time, is the crisis, the absolute turning point in the plot which divides the reign of law and promise from the reign of grace and fulfillment and assures the happy outcome. The visible denouement of the plot, however, awaits Christ's second Advent, which will bring an immediate restoration of lost happiness on earth. His reign will be followed, at an unknown but appointed moment, by the abrupt termination of this world and of time and their replacement, for all who shall be deemed worthy in the Last Judgment, by a heavenly kingdom in eternity.[26]

The chief "consequence" of this vision of history is its effect on Christian autobiography. Abrams notes that Augustine's "moral psychology" is

> very different from representative classical treatments of self-reliance, self-continuity, and the rational weighing of alternatives; it is, however, entirely consonant with the crises, cataclysms, and right-angled changes of the Christian pattern of history.[27]

Augustine's *Confessions*, in turn, is the antecedent for countless subsequent works, including one Abrams has no occasion to cite: John Wesley's *Journal*.

A recent editor calls attention to Wesleyan echoes of the *Confessions* and rightly compares the Methodist's "Aldersgate experience" with that of Augustine in the Milanese garden.[28] St. Paul is an influence, too, (as are Wesley's Moravian friends) with the net result that Wesley professes his belief in almost instantaneous conversion. He begins by asserting his reluctance to accept such an idea: "I could not understand how this faith should be given in a moment: how a man could at once be thus turned from darkness to light, from sin and misery to righteousness and joy in the Holy Ghost."[29] But upon re-reading Scripture, he finds, to his "utter astonishment . . . scarce any instances there of other than *instantaneous* conversions: scarce any so slow as that of St. Paul, who was three days in the pangs of the new birth."[30] After meeting living witnesses who testify that "God *can* (at least, if he *does* not always) give that faith whereof cometh salvation in a moment, as lightning falling from heaven,"[31] Wesley is ready for the conversion that occurs with memorable specificity on May 24, 1738, at "about a quarter before nine [p.m.]"[32] This passage is drawn from the most influential, but not the only, record of Wesley's life. And, as his editor points out, the discrepancies among them suggest that this version "was carefully reconstructed . . . as a dramatic story."[33] The exigencies of narrative, it seems, are partly responsible for the emphatic and temporally precise nature of the event; they gratify Wesley's need to view his conversion retrospectively as a sudden event. The Aldersgate experience is thus conventionalized in exactly the way Abrams leads one to expect.

One makes this same discovery when reading secular autobiographies. Great crises and readjustments of self-perception tend to be highly localized. The autobiographical shock may be as gentle as Wordsworth's discovery that he is "changed . . . from what [he] was when first / [He] came among these hills"[34] or as painful as the news of a death which makes Tennyson feel that "all he was is overworn."[35] But the transition from "sad perplexity" to joy,[36] or bereavement to faith is securely linked with a diarist's precision to a specific time and place: the banks of the Wye during a tour, July 13, 1798, or the lawn at Somersby one summer evening while reading the "letters of the dead."[37] Diogenes Teufelsdröckh's "baphometic fire-baptism" occurs in the space of a question while walking the Rue Saint-Thomas de l'Enfer;[38] Mill's recovery is signalled by the shedding of tears over a passage of Marmontel's "Memoires."[39]

But an explanation by convention and precedent only initiates the subject of Browning's preference for sudden conversions. His insistence on the abruptness of major transformations warrants further consideration, particularly since Browning knows—the tradition notwithstanding—that instantaneous change is psychologically suspect. He is well aware that complete renewal or the choice of a life work does not occur in a flash. He knows, too, that such discoveries are the result of gradual analysis and dawning self-awareness. In *Paracelsus*, for example, the hero's choice of vocation has been patiently evaluated; he has explored the depth of his being in order to validate his commitment to the pursuit of knowledge:

> What fairer seal
> Shall I require to my authentic mission
> Than this fierce energy?—this instinct striving
> Because its nature is to strive.   (I. 333–36).

And yet, eschewing all subtlety, Browning launches his hero's career with a miraculous event. Paracelsus insists, very literally, that the "selection of [his] lot" (I. 293) is the result of a divine commission. Like the patriarchs, the young Samuel, and St. Paul, Paracelsus has heard God speak; "A still voice from without said—'Seest thou not, / Desponding child, whence spring defeat and loss?" (I. 513–14). This calling abruptly initiates the whole man. And while Paracelsus does not follow the Biblical convention of taking a new name to signify his

new identity, he considers himself, as of this instant, a changed
creature:

> As he spoke, I was endued
> With comprehension and a steadfast will;
> And when he ceased, my brow was sealed his own.
> If there took place no special change in me,
> How comes it all things wore a different hue
> Thenceforward?—pregnant with vast consequence,
> Teeming with grand result, loaded with fate?   (I. 546–52).

What is of interest in Paracelsus' pairing of introspective and theo-
phanic explanations is the equation implied. A young man's emerging
sense of purpose is represented as a divine episode. Commitment is
regarded as an interior state, but also as a response to an external
stimulus. The reader wonders what satisfaction Browning finds in this
analogy and why a process is condensed into an event. The poem itself
provides a partial answer.

Although Browning works with the convention of sudden voca-
tion, he rejects the usual implication of finality. Paracelsus' calling
is assumed throughout the poem to be valid, but the security it confers,
the consequence of divine selection, is problematic. In this regard, the
poem can be read as a comment on the theology of the covenant. The
miraculous nature of the event is in keeping with the traditional idea
of Justification; it virtually dramatizes the maxim that "the New
Creature, being a Divine Thing, cannot be educed of Natural Princi-
ples."[40] But if Paracelsus has been truly chosen by God, he ought,
according to the Calvinist view of "effectual calling" to be "stainless of
all sin, / Preserved and sanctified by inward light" (V. 247–48). On
this matter, Browning's psychology and covenantal theology diverge.
Paracelsus is obviously not sanctified and Browning clearly has his
own ideas about effectuality. He assumes that a single event can
transform, but cannot fix, the personality; and he shapes Paracelsus'
life as a series of confrontations with exactly this fact. In each book the
mage tries to comprehend his calling and is repeatedly baffled by the
indeterminacy of his own personality. Browning's belief, expressed in
this poem as a whole, is that an abrupt change of consciousness may be
undeniably real, but that it is not necessarily conclusive. An event may
be profoundly compelling without being defining.

The poem also considers and explicitly denies the possibility of sudden change on a grand racial scale. The young Paracelsus has a millenarian confidence that humanity can be universally and abruptly converted. Fondly supposing that mankind's "full maturity" is imminently attainable, he longs to expedite the process of history and

> one day, one moment's space,
> Change man's condition, push each slumbering claim
> Of mastery o'er the elemental world
> At once to full maturity. (V. 821 24).

He soon discovers that "one moment's space" cannot accommodate such transformation. The sad truth that even a lifetime is insufficient accounts in part for his growing bitterness. Only with his final vision does Paracelsus learn that his expectations were naively wrong-headed. The divine plan is not climactic but evolutionary, providing for the ongoing completion of man's being.

It is indicative of Browning's attitude, however, that this lesson needs to be repeated in other poems and that the dreamily millenarian hero of *Sordello* must receive similar instruction. The thrust of Book V is to create in Sordello a realistic understanding of the slow rise of civilization and the sluggish pace of human events. But even as Browning educates his hero, his own desire to coerce time influences his choice of metaphors. His wish to subdue reality to man's will finds expression—almost subversively—in images of crisis. When considering the interminable rivalry between Papal and civil authority, for example, he visualizes Hildebrand's long struggle against lay investiture as a single vibration in stone:

> A staggering—a shock—
> What's mere sand is demolished, while the rock
> Endures: a column of black fiery dust
> Blots heaven. (V. 155–58).

Such an image can be accommodated logically—the slow work of time may reach precipitous accomplishment—but the passage is best regarded as an indication of Browning's preference for crisis. In the very act of reconciling his hero to the gradualism of history, Browning becomes excited by the prospect of a condensed and energetic culmination.

It should be noted parenthetically that a fondness for drastic change is so basic to Browning's sensibility that even his landscapes are instantly alterable. They rarely serve as emblems of stately cosmic purpose, but seem the product of a kind of licensed poetic catastrophism. The succession of night and day is typically represented as one more startling event in an abruptly changeful world. The sun rises "of a sudden" and sets with "violent" drama:

>   when delicate evening dies,
> And you follow its spent sun's pallid range,
> There's a shoot of colour startles the skies
> With sudden, violent change,—   ("Gold Hair" (ll. 23–25).

The stars "outburst" upon the night, and moonlight causes "the startled little waves" to "leap / In fiery ringlets from their sleep" ("Meeting at Night," ll. 3–4). The rotation of seasons is every bit as spectacular. In "Up at a Villa" summer arrives "all at once; / In a day he leaps complete with a few strong April suns" (ll. 21–22); and in "A Lovers' Quarrel," winter is signaled not by a gradual drop in temperature, but by stunning unseasonable cold, "the warning slash / Of his driver's-lash" (ll. 129–30). Even the mountains, forests, and streams "thrust," "heave," "rush," and transform themselves as if the natural laws of cause and effect were accelerated or suspended.[41] This obvious preference for the cataclysmic and unnatural in nature again raises the issue of Browning's love of right-angled events. He knows full well that natural changes are not literally the work of seconds. He knows, too, that the self—individually or collectively—cannot be transformed in a grandly unexpected rush of awareness. Why then does he cling to the myth of "one moment's space"?

The answer lies partly in the dramatic appeal of suddenness and partly in the fact that unexpectedness is the temporal equivalent of luxurious excess. For Browning, a joy is intensified if it occurs fortuitously. In the second year, for example, of his carefully negotiated visits to Elizabeth, he dreams of encountering her by accident:

> I fancy myself meeting you on "the stairs"—stairs and passages
> generally, and galleries (ah, those indeed!—) all, with their picturesque

accidents, of landing-places, and spiral heights & depths, and sudden turns and visions of half open doors into what Quarles calls "mollitious chambers"—and above all, *landing-places*—they are my heart's delight—I would come upon you unaware on a landing-place in my next dream![42]

More important than even the drama or pleasure of the unexpected is the symbolic value of a clearly defined temporal space. Underlying the myth of instantaneous conversion is man's need both to organize the past and to obtain relief from its burdens. The tendency to condense an evolutionary process by declaring a precise boundary between old and new bespeaks a desire to seal off the history that might cause pain. The more clearly defined the crisis, the more convincing the barrier. Emotionally intense and temporally discrete, it permits a liberating discontinuity while at the same time it orders the life before and after.

Another factor behind Browning's use of this myth is the traditional association of spontaneity and authenticity. Both the religious myth of sudden conversion and the Romantic myth of unpremeditated creativity suggest that the "product," whether it be a renovated identity or a lyric ode, is the expression of the truest self. When Saul is struck by God on the road to Damascus, he rises up a new man and a genuine Christian. When Augustine's "iron will" capitulates, he tells God gratefully, "Thou didst again place me before myself" (VIII. 7). Both cases imply that the convert has achieved integrity and that the true identity has been released from the superficiality of sin or error. The passage from old to new corresponds to a vertical passage through the layers of self. A similar notion underlies Wordsworth's definition of poetry:

> I have said that poetry is the spontaneous overflow of powerful feelings: it takes its origin from emotion recollected in tranquillity: the emotion is contemplated till, by a species of re-action, the tranquillity gradually disappears, and an emotion, kindred to that which was before the subject of contemplation, is gradually produced, and does itself actually exist in the mind. In this mood successful composition generally begins, and in a mood similar to this it is carried on.[43]

"Contemplation" recovers and even enlarges emotion, but the "origin" of poetry is urgent or "powerful" feeling. And, as the metaphor of "overflow" suggests, the source of authentic utterance is deeply interior; true art emanates, like Coleridge's "Dejection: An Ode," from the passion "whose fountains are within."[44] Wordsworth does not, to be precise, affirm that "composition" is spontaneous—though even he can entitle an occasional work "Extempore Effusion"—but his careful distinctions are not always maintained by the next generation of writers. "If Poetry comes not as naturally as the Leaves to a tree," writes Keats, "it had better not come at all."[45] And when Shelley hails the "Skylark" as "thou"

> That from Heaven, or near it,
>   Pourest thy full heart
> In profuse strains of unpremeditated art,

the relation between sincerity and immediacy is literally and firmly established.[46] The true poet's song is to be impromptu; and poetic expression, like conversion, is looked upon as the abrupt revelation of self.[47] Browning accepts this equation of suddenness and sincerity and makes it uniquely his own. In his poetry, gradual change often implies adaptation and accommodation. Suddenness, however, seems to leave no opportunity for mediation and serves as a metaphor for integrity. It is by this route that Browning comes to discredit the monotonous, as in "Pictor Ignotus" and "The Statue and the Bust," and to value impulsiveness instead.

This fertile association of the honest and the abrupt has ramifications not only for Browning's narration and imagery but for his style as well. He gladly explores the possibilities of the inadvertent digression, the blurted confidence, and the shocked response. Spontaneity, to be sure, is no guarantee of profundity. An impulsive judgment—like Browning's hasty opinion of Dante in a letter to Elizabeth—may be rashly inept, a burst of jejune sentiment to be recanted with a painterly metaphor: "Now you see how I came to say some nonsense . . . some desperate splash . . . for the beginning of my picture. . . ."[48] Nevertheless, Browning instinctively values "splashes" and "first fine careless rapture" ("Home-Thoughts, from Abroad," 1.16). This attitude creates some vivid exchanges in his correspondence with Elizabeth, for she has the frustrating habit of crossing out sentences and thereby depriving him of her initial, unguarded thoughts:

[W]hy, why, do you blot out, in that unutterably provoking manner, whole lines, not to say words, in your letters—(and in the criticism on the "Duchess")—if it is a fact that you have a second thought, does it cease to be as genuine a fact, that first thought you please to efface? Why give a thing and take a thing? Is there no significance in putting on record that your first impression was to a certain effect and your next to a certain other, perhaps completely opposite one? If any proceeding of yours could go near to deserve that harsh word "impertinent" which you have twice, in speech and writing, been pleased to apply to your observations on me,—certainly *this* does go as near as can be. . . .[49]

Convinced that the "first impression" is a "genuine fact," Elizabeth yields on this matter of blotting. Henceforth, she resorts to a censoring line—"to prove I have a conscience"[50]—and abandons the obliterating cancellation. The point to be made here is that what the suitor demands of his love, the poet supplies for his speakers. They burst out with what Elizabeth would call "unwary sentences,"[51] and their creator clearly relishes their genuineness and texture. The Italian, for example, is restored by unsummoned memories and concludes his monologue with exclamatory vigor: "So much for idle wishing—how / It steals the time! To business now" ("The Italian in England," ll. 161–62). The loyal huntsman of "The Flight of the Duchess" has long kept his lady's secret but now feels vividly garrulous relief:

> I always wanted to make a clean breast of it:
> And now it is made—why, my heart's-blood, that went trickle,
> Trickle but anon, in such muddy driblets,
> Is pumped up brisk now.   (ll. 848–51).

And Caponsacchi, stunned by the news of Pompilia's stabbing, turns on the judges with surging indignation:

>   now of a sudden here you summon me
> To take the intelligence from just—your lips
> You, Judge Tommati, who then tittered most,—
> . . . .
> Pompilia is bleeding out her life belike,
> Gasping away the latest breath of all,
> This minute, while I talk—not while you laugh?
>   (VI. 32–34, 61–63).

Browning loves human voices and uses all the resources of syntax, pace, juncture, and sound to capture the effusiveness of unguarded utterance or the restraint of manipulated and manipulating speech. Compare the monosyllabic alliteration of Caliban's high, choppy glee—"to talk about him vexes—ha, / Could He but know! and time to vex is now" (ll. 17–18)—with the flowing euphony of the Duke's financial diplomacy:

> The Count your Master's known munificence
> Is ample warrant that no just pretence
> Of mine for dowry will be disallowed.   (ll. 50–52).

The smaller differences between the values of stressed and unstressed syllables in the latter's speech cause his lines to disappear into polysyllables that have their own momentum.

The assumption that style is itself a kind of meaning underlies Browning's greatest monologues. His love of highly textured utterance derives from his belief that man's use of language has much to do with the conditions of his soul. There are, of course, no simple rules whereby he translates a set of personality traits into a given character's verbal habits. Browning's art depends not on a system, but on the knowledge that the creative impulse is as unique as it is universal. Anything man forms, he in some degree informs. Sentences, like other products of human consciousness, necessarily bear their creator's stamp. In addition to their speaker's intended meanings, they exhibit by their sound and shape the control he exercises over that meaning. A style that is conspicuously polished raises questions about the speaker's motive: perhaps the meaning he glosses over is incriminating. By the same token, a lack or disruption of high style may suggest truthful, or at least unrehearsed, utterance. The reader of a monologue must, therefore, be alert to caesuras, alliteration, and syntax; for— "style or no style" ("Two Poets of Croisic," 1. 304)—these technicalities are Browning's way of revealing his speakers' personalities.

In the early poems, as one might suspect, the voices are not particularly rich, and the correlation between the rush of sincere emotion and the impetuous flow of words is rather naively—some would say spasmodically—handled. There are too many overwrought exclamations—"O God, where do they tend—these struggling aims"

(*Pauline* 1. 811)—and startlingly ineffective transitions—"I paused again: a change was coming—came" (*Pauline* 1. 394).[52] And while frequent shifts of theme can convey the urgency of new or tentative feelings, they can also leave an unfortunately diffused impression on the reader. At one point Pauline's poet discusses what he thinks is his "rudely" impulsive style:

> I must not think, lest this new impulse die
> In which I trust; I have no confidence:
> So, I will sing on fast as fancies come;
> Rudely, the verse being as the mood it paints.   (ll. 256–59).

This apology is meant to place the poem in the Shelleyan category of "unbidden hymns," and yet the lines themselves lack Shelley's breathlessness and have very little rhythmic surge. Paracelsus struggles with his new impulses in a slightly different but no more effective way. Victimized by his rage, Paracelsus finds relief by bullying his auditor:

> you . . . are clearly
> Guiltless of understanding more, a whit,
> The subject than your stool.   (III. 167–69).

And he too invokes the principle of spontaneity, explaining that "this morning's strange encounter" (III. 374) is the cause of his excited discourse. Under extreme emotional pressure, he speaks without forethought, unguardedly saying "what comes uppermost" (III. 372). Despite the apology, and despite, too, the "harshness and abruptness" George Henry Lewes complained of, Paracelsus' syntax is emphatically *not* spontaneous.[53] His use of inversion and suspension is uncharacteristic of speakers under pressure.

In each of these poems, what is meant to sound earnestly or painfully effusive strikes some readers as insincere. J. S. Mill, for example, was unconvinced by *Pauline*.[54] Mistrustful of the speaker's self-accusations, Mill was also annoyed by the conclusion of the poem. The triply renewed young man maintains that he ends his song "in perfect joy" (1. 994) and yet fears that he will relapse into his former self-loathing and again "deny, decry, despise" (1. 991). This inconsistency so exasperated Mill that he grumbled "Bad luck to him!" in the margins of his review copy. But the speaker's ambivalence is not, in itself, a sign of instability; his mixed conclusion reflects the fact that a spiritual event may have a lasting influence without being definitive. The speaker feels menaced by the return of aimlessness and aridity because conversions are provisional.

That a reader can even question the sincerity of Pauline's poet is an ironic indication of the poem's inadequacy, for Browning puts his speaker through all the right motions and certainly intends his confession to be candidly forthright. In keeping with his promise to "strip [his] mind bare" (l. 260), he eagerly discusses both the historical and psychological origins of his personality. On the one hand, he describes the emotions "connected with [his] early life" (l. 137) and traces his interior growth from the "first dawn of life" (l. 318) up to the present. On the other hand, he unveils, in a much-quoted section of self-analysis, the "first elements" (l. 260) of his being:

> I am made up of an intensest life,
> Of a most clear idea of consciousness
> Of self, distinct from all its qualities,
>
> . . . .
> But linked, in me, to self-supremacy,
> Existing as a centre to all things,
>
> . . . .
> And to a principle of restlessness
> Which would be all, have, see, know, taste, feel all—
> This is myself. . . .
>
> . . . .
> . . . of powers the only one
> Which marks me—an imagination which
> Has been a very angel, coming not
> In fitful visions but beside me ever
> And never failing me.   (ll. 268–287).

Both his intensity and his dual method recall the work of Rousseau. Although it cannot be shown that Browning read the *Confessions* prior to *Pauline*, it has been suspected before that "the archetypal romantic confession . . . was also in Browning's mind as a model."[55] The similarity begins with Rousseau's famous first page and his declared intention of completely exposing himself: "Je dirai hautement: voilà ce que j'ai fait, ce que j'ai pensé, ce que je fus. J'ai dit le bien et le mal avec la même franchise."[56] It continues throughout as he offers a hitherto unprecedented account of his development—"c'est la chaîne des sentiments qui ont marqué la succession de mon être"—commencing with his earliest emotions—"Telle furent les premières affections de mon entrée à la vie."[57] Other features that could have influenced Browning include the care with which Rousseau traces the origin of self-awareness—"c'est le temps d'où je date sans interruption la conscience de moi-même"[58]—his comments on his power of imagina- tion—"Dans cette étrange situation mon inquiète imagination prit un parti qui me suava de moi-même et calma ma naissante sensualité"[59]— and his frequent efforts to summarize his temperament—"Deux chose presque inalliables s'unissent en moi sans que j'en puisse concevoir la maniere: un tempérament très ardent, des passions vives, impétueuses, et des idées lentes à naitre, embarrassées, et qui ne se présentent jamais qu'après coup."[60] But more significant perhaps than any single aspect of Rousseau's self-analysis is the pervasive assumption underlying the *Confessions*. Rousseau believes he discerns his true self; Lionel Trilling sums the matter up with the remark that "on his pre-eminence in sincerity Rousseau is uncompromising."[61] In this Pauline's poet resembles him most; he too believes in, tries to reveal and to recover his essential self. The reason his confession is not wholly convincing is the poem's stylistic immaturity. The various expressions of hope and dread do not emanate from a believable speaker; the voice in its many moods remains undifferentiated. The young man is in what is actually a very interesting condition, but the poetry is blandly uncompelling. Browning learns his craft, however, and a look at "The Bishop Orders his Tomb" shows how he manages a voice that is erratically complex and how, stylistically, he creates the impression of spontaneous utterance.

The sensual bishop has at least two distinct voices. A skilled preacher, he moralizes with polished authority. In one passage, the habit of repetition carries him across neatly iambic lines to a demure rhetorical question, while pseudo-logic (as, so, thence) and easy parataxis (and, and, and) give his comments clarity and continuity:

What's done is done, and she is dead beside,
Dead long ago, and I am Bishop since,

> And as she died so must we die ourselves,
> And thence ye may perceive the world's a dream.
> Life, how and what is it?   (ll. 6–10).

In numerous shorter passages this same voice intones aphorisms in solemn end-stops:

> Vanity, saith the preacher, vanity!   (l.1).

> Swift as a weaver's shuttle fleet our years:
> Man goeth to the grave, and where is he?   (ll. 51–52).

> Evil and brief hath been my pilgrimage.   (l. 101).[62]

But in his private life the prelate is fiercely competitive. When this instinct asserts itself, his meditation on peace degenerates rapidly into a curse. The voice of the inner man has a very different and stylistically compulsive kind of authority:

>   Peace, peace seems all.
> Saint Praxed's ever was the church for peace;
> And so, about this tomb of mine. I fought
> With tooth and nail to save my niche, ye know:
> —Old Gandolf cozened me, despite my care;
> Shrewd was that snatch from out the corner South
> He graced his carrion with, God curse the same!   (ll. 13–19).

The turn is abrupt—"and so." Repetition is eschewed as he goes directly to the point "about this tomb." Line 15, charged with vehemence, is heavily enjambed while the caesuras are very emphatic. The phrasing—no longer a pre-measured five beats—lurches, suggesting the obtrusiveness and even the obsessiveness of his rivalry with "Old Gandolf." The harsh, sometimes snarling, diction—*cozened, carrion, curse, despite, shrewd, snatch*—of this grammatically transitionless burst of malice gives the reader a stylistic as well as a moral shock. This latter disruptive voice is clearly more authentic than the smoothly cadenced and professional. And the rivalry of the voices is both the form and the meaning of the poem; it makes the division in the bishop's personality convincing.

The intense drama of "The Bishop Orders his Tomb" indicates, by way of contrast, how uniform the voice in *Pauline* actually is and how it fails to register changes in mood. As soon as one recognizes this limitation, however, the speaker's avowals of confessional urgency can be accepted without challenge. The most important fact which then emerges is that his speech is the result of a "new impulse" (l. 256). His confession is like that of a religious convert insofar as it ratifies a significant change. In his case public utterance is especially important since the fall he has recovered from is, in part, a poet's fall into silence. His outpouring to Pauline is a sign of artistic regeneration and the first fruit of his literary awakening.

This particular kind of fall, the failure of aesthetic desire, recurs in Browning's poetry and is treated somewhat idiosyncratically. Not simply an aesthetic problem, it is a moral failing as well; and the withdrawn artist is a reprehensible figure. When Pauline's frustrated poet gives up trying to share his millenarian dreams, there is a decidedly selfish element in his decision to "let them fade / Untold" (ll. 520–21). His resolve is not merely the opposite of impulsiveness, it is the aesthetic equivalent of miserliness. To remain inarticulate is shameful self-indulgence; "And my soul's idol ever whispers me / To dwell with him and his unhonoured song" (ll. 540–41). A similar association of ideas occurs in *Paracelsus* where Aprile, a potential poet, suffers the torment of "unexerted powers" (II. 320). He is guilty of what Browning elsewhere describes as the "primitive folly . . . of desiring to do nothing when [one] cannot do all; seeing nothing, getting, enjoying nothing, where there is no seeing & enjoying wholly."[63] In a series of self-revealing questions, Aprile asks if Paracelsus has ever been startled by the murmuring "of darkling mortals famished for one ray / Of thy so-hoarded luxury of light" (II. 596–97). Silence, conceived in these terms, is misanthropic; and Aprile's buried assumption is that the failure to articulate is like a refusal to love. His comparison suggests the similarity between the artist's and the lover's relation with reality. Both require uncautious commitment to someone or something beyond the self. And both, for this reason, are more than a little frightening. The self, according to Aprile, fears the constriction of intense focus and the surrender of emotional dedication. Herein lie the cause of hesitation and the source of Browning's disapprobation. The reserve of the silent or unloving man is self-solicitous; his inhibition is a defensive strategy.

For the fullest early treatment of this theme one must look to *Sordello*, for that much-revised poem deals extensively with the problem of self-expression. Sordello is perceptually well-endowed; his is the "flesh that amply lets in loveliness / At eye and ear" (I. 478–79). Blessed with the sympathetic power Keats once called the "camelion" (sic) faculty,[64] he can penetrate "earth's simplest combination stampt / With individuality" (I. 543–44). Thus gifted, he is "equal to being all" (I. 548) and capable of imaginative infinitude. But Sordello is also a lamentable narcissist whose every encounter with reality is cause for self-congratulation. The discovery of "the poppy's red effrontery" (I. 706) or the bravery of a hero involves the simultaneous discovery that beauty and bravery are qualities known to him by his own soul's anticipation. He

> eagerly looks, too,
> On beauty. . .
> Proclaims each new revealment born a twin
> With a distinctest consciousness within,
> Referring still the quality, now first
> Revealed to [his] own soul.   (I. 523–28).

He is undeniably correct in his belief that "revealments" are reflexive, but his appreciation is too egotistically exclusive. He nearly forgets that exterior reality is the ground of discovery and that sympathy is a process of dialectic. The aesthetic consequences of his disproportionate self-regard are predictable enough. Art proves inadequate to the needs of his hungry ego; and when experience teaches him that song cannot reveal the full majesty of his soul, he gives up altogether. Alone in his retreat, he exhibits the same ungenerous blend of feelings as his predecessors. Determined to "slumber in the solitude / Thus reached," (I. 555–56) he resolves never again to "task [himself] for mankind's good" (I. 556). Eventually Sordello reconceives the function of art, but the point of this first episode is crucial and it is one that Browning makes repeatedly throughout his career. Self-expression cannot be the artist's primary objective; for if it is, every aesthetic act will disappoint him. Every specific creation will misrepresent the infinitude of his soul and leave him "remote as ever from the self-display / He meant to compass" (II. 651–52). As frustrations accumulate, the artist will become guarded, cautious, and increasingly selfish. The desire for infinite and fully simultaneous self-expression is thus perversely debilitating. A refined form of egomania, it undermines the very process of art. It makes the self unsympathetic, incapable of attending to the object world, and painfully aware of its own longing restlessness. In short, the goal of authentic revelation is inhibiting. The Romantic achievement, needless to say, stands in permanent rebuttal to Browning's conclusions. But they are true to his own youthful experience and their assertion is necessary for his artistic growth. Attracted and yet intimidated by the imperative to be egotistically sublime or subjectively vatic, Browning struggles in *Sordello* to complete the emancipation begun in *Pauline* and to work himself free of the Romantic aesthetic.

The victim of inhibition does not, in Browning's poetry, always resort to silence; it is the most drastic, but not the only, response to frustration. Compromises are possible, and Browning is as interested in the formal as in the psychological dynamics of embarrassment. If self-expression is too frightening, the timid artist can resort to sanctioned repetition. The painter of "Pictor Ignotus," for example, dreads going forth, "I, in each new picture" (l. 26). Protecting himself even at the cost of his own art, he offers the world uninspired holy pictures endlessly reproducing "the same series, Virgin, Babe, and Saint, / With the same, cold, calm beautiful regard" (ll. 60–61). He finds monotony an effective strategy; such pictures do not engage or seriously exercise his talent. Their inadequacies, he assumes, are those of the genre and do not personally humiliate him. He welcomes the conventions that insure his obscurity. The morbidity of his conclusion —"So, die my pictures! surely, gently die!" (l. 69)—makes it abundantly clear that Browning finds such cowardly self-effacement deplorable; deliberate mediocrity is the wrong way to alleviate the burden of "self-display."

The painter's monologue makes the valid point, however, that the problem of self-expression is, in part, technical. The distance between the artist and his artifact is not absolute, and what may appear to be matters of purely formal choice are sometimes ways of adjusting this psychological distance. Just such a decision is dramatized in Part III of *Pippa Passes*. Under the influence of Pippa's song, the young sculptor Jules resolves to "begin art afresh" (II. 318). He suddenly dreads the technical dexterity that masks severe inadequacy, the easy mastery that can "reproduce with a fatal expertness the ancient types" (IV. 53–4). The statues that were his pride now seem so "paltry" he rejects the security that the "Pictor Ignotus" welcomes. Rather than remain burdened with the past, he chooses to make new demands on himself; "he will turn painter instead of sculptor'" (IV. 57). Unwilling to hide behind mastered conventions, he commits himself to resistant new materials. This decision not only rescues Jules from his dull achievements, it solves the problem of aesthetic inhibition. The challenge of a new medium requires enormous expenditures of energy. New formal problems become injunctions that command fascinated and unselfconscious effort. Most important of all, the commitment to an unmastered craft makes a saving difference in the artist's sense of purpose. Self-engagement rather than self-expression becomes the basis of his relationship with his art. Jules's decision to turn painter embodies one of the great discoveries of Browning's poetry: the inhibiting burden of self-display can be lifted; the self-expressive goals which prevent their own accomplishment can be reconceived.

Art history corroborates Browning's insight on this matter with well-known examples of commitments to new media. Two of these, Raphael's "century of sonnets" and Dante's effort to "paint an angel," are cited in "One Word More" (ll. 5, 32) to make much the same point as Jules's episode. Greater artists than Jules, Raphael and Dante seek, nonetheless, to be freed technically from the "art that's turned his nature" (l. 64). Each wishes to speak more directly than usual—"to find his love a language / Fit and fair and simple and sufficient" (ll. 61–62)—and turns deliberately to a problematic art. Such a self-imposed challenge puts "to proof art alien to the artist's" and releases new aesthetic ardor (l. 69). Browning then advances a modified version of this strategy; if complete changes of media are not possible, perhaps shifts of genre may be effective:

> He who works in fresco, steals a hair-brush,
> Curbs the liberal hand, subservient proudly,
> Cramps his spirit, crowds its all in little,
> Makes a strange art of an art familiar,
> Fills his lady's missal-marge with flowerets.
> He who blows thro' bronze, may breathe thro' silver,
> Fitly serenade a slumbrous princess.   (ll. 121–27).

The strategy has dangers, of course. If inhibition is no longer a problem, failure is. But Browning is more comfortable, morally, with the idea of depletion than with that of hoarding. There is a significant difference between the exhaustion that a Jules might eventually suffer and the enervation of Pauline's poet, Aprile, or Sordello. The equivalent of Roland's weariness, Jules's aesthetic fatigue would be the honorable result of unreserved commitment. Browning is sympathetic with, but not pleased by, the complaints of his retired poets *in potentia*:

> I have nursed up energies,
> They will prey on me.   (*Pauline*, ll. 481–82).

> I could not curb
> My yearnings, . . .
> . . .but neglected all the means
> Of realizing even the frailest joy,
> Gathering no fragments to appease my want,
> Yet nursing up that want till thus I die.
>   (*Paracelsus*, II. 388–92, Aprile's lines).

Browning suspects that real talents, if hoarded, wane and diminish. Genius, he says, is a wild swan that suffers change when captured, a chained God who grows "less radiant" (*Pauline*, l. 115).

Jules's discovery that exertion, not revelation, underlies the intimacy of artist and artifact can be related to the development of Browning's own aesthetic, but it is helpful first to take another brief look at *Sordello*. The poem is famous for its obscurity, and the short introductory letter to Milsand is probably more quoted than the work itself. In it Browning says, "My stress lay on the incidents in the development of a soul; little else is worth study."[65] One assumes that this statement applies to the protagonist and is not surprised to find that the poem treats Sordello's aesthetic conversion. But to see exactly how his renewal is accomplished one must look to the speaker who tells Sordello's story. An artist himself, the poet-narrator deals brusquely with his hero and is frankly uneasy about the course his story takes. It is soon apparent that he is less interested in mediating between the historical Sordello and the audience than in using the poem *Sordello* to discover some truth for himself. The narrator, it turns out, is in crisis. In Book III he drops Sordello's story altogether and speaks of his difficulties in writing the poem. He, like his hero, is in danger of becoming one of Browning's silent poets. His aesthetic commitments are so uncertain that he doesn't know how to clarify Sordello's or even finish the poem. But Browning allows him his own conversion experience and makes Book III his confession. There, a vision of the human race as a "sad dishevelled" woman comes to him (III. 696); and he realizes, in the words in Browning's own paraphrase, that she is meant to "prick up my republicanism."[66]

> [A]s I stopped my task awhile, the sad
> Dishevelled form, wherein I put mankind
> To come at times and keep my pact in mind,
> Renewed me.   (III. 968–71).

Henceforth, the narrator will serve this "care-bit erased / Broken-up" female by enlisting his art in the service of common humanity (III. 747–48). When the vision ends, his personal decision quickly becomes his protagonist's, and Sordello finds that he too must accept the artist's "portion in the common lot" (III. 807). The reader is tempted at this point to relax: the concept of art which emerges is familiar. The once silent Sordello now wants to become one of the Shelleyan legislators of mankind—one of the company of lawmakers, prophets, and artists who organize and share significant perceptions of reality. He wants to be the kind of poet described in Browning's own "Essay on Shelley," "the poet of loftier vision" who can "lift his fellows, with their half apprehensions up to his own sphere."[67] As the poem unravels, the narrator gives his hero the chance to live the role of the poet-seer. But Sordello is unable to turn his humanitarian altruism to account. After many twists and turns of plot—which need not be summarized here —Sordello simply falls dead. Loyal to the mission of prophecy, Sordello nevertheless dies without speaking. His commitment is vitiated and his silence is final. This lame, hardly inevitable conclusion may strike the reader as mere ineptitude on the young Browning's part, but it is something more. The poem's conclusion is a comment on Sordello's conception of the poet.

    The narrator's earlier discussion of the genesis of Sordello's story indicates that he consciously controls the outcome of the poem. The conclusion is his; as narrative maker, he decides that Sordello shall not survive his aesthetic commitment. He allows Sordello to choose, but not to live, the role they both admire. The narrator, in other words, can conceive of the prophetic mission, but he cannot conceive of his hero's actually pursuing it. The entire poem is a sardonic, tacit and clear admission by the narrator that the most exalted poetic role is, for him, unrealizable.

A strange, difficult poem, *Sordello* ought to be read as a literary elegy. A long unwilling farewell, it laments the futility of once-cherished poetic aims. Read in conjunction with Browning's other poems on aesthetic inhibition, it clarifies Jules's achievement in *Pippa Passes*. Sordello's story rules out, while Jules's defines, possible artistic commitments. And although Jules is a sculptor turned painter, his conversion reflects lessons learned in Browning's poetic apprenticeship. His resolve to "begin Art afresh" (II. 318) is his author's, and his dedication to a new medium reflects Browning's own practice. After the veiled autobiography and aesthetic wrestling of the early narratives, Browning changes genre. He alleviates the anxiety of "self-display" and the burden of conscious prophecy by lavishing his talent upon prelates, lovers, artists and questors. Gifted like all his young heroes with the ability to penetrate "earth's simplest combination stampt / With individuality" (*Sordello* I. 543–44), he chooses the individuality of others as his medium. By this stroke he loses his inhibition and is free neither to hoard nor to compromise but to spend himself generously, expressing the sensibility of Saul, Andrea, Karshish, Lippo, Caliban, Roland and a host of others.

Often, but not always, the new medium is the flow of words as these others speak for themselves. And in the dramatic monologue as Browning develops it, the central interest is not simply what his characters say—or don't say—to their auditors, but what they are willing to disclose to themselves. In this way, Browning shifts the burden of self-expression onto his speakers and combines it with that of self-knowledge. Browning can say, therefore, with Shakespeare, "Mine remains the unproffered soul" ("At the 'Mermaid,' " 1. 28) and yet know that the most intimate of human tensions is the major subject of his impersonal art. His characters who speak "in the confessing vein" are often tempted to misrepresent themselves. Browning is well aware that the reluctant confessant is not likely to fall silent; on the contrary, his inhibition is manifested in evasive manipulations of fact. But if the individual's scrutiny is honest, if he is unafraid of true self-display, Browning allows him to be saved, motivated, or transformed according to his need.

2

"In Thunder From the Stars": Rescue and Renewal

Browning's fascination with sudden crises often finds expression in tales of deliverance. Rescues abound in his poetry; and the exertions of his mystic, historic, and romance saviors—including the gypsy queen of "The Flight of the Duchess," the priest Caponsacchi of *The Ring and the Book*, the boy David of "Saul," and even Bishop Blougram— are both energetic and varied. The first such episode occurs in *Pauline*, where, with an eclecticism that serves him well, Browning refers simultaneously to Caravaggio's *Andromeda* and Shelley's "Ode to the West Wind." The speaker's mode of address is only vaguely reminiscent of Shelley's invocational style, but his details of "spread" and "lifted" hair, "red" beam, and "storm leaves" are clearly borrowed from the Sun-Treader's "hectic red" leaves and approaching storm clouds "spread . . . like the bright hair uplifted from the head / Of some fierce maenad."[1]

> Andromeda!
> . . .so beautiful
> With her fixed eyes, earnest and still, and hair
> Lifted and spread by the salt-sweeping breeze,
> And one red beam, all the storm leaves in heaven,

> Resting upon her eyes and hair, such hair,
> As she awaits the snake on the wet beach
> By the dark rock and the white wave just breaking
> At her feet; quite naked and alone; a thing
> I doubt not, nor fear for, secure some god
> To save will come in thunder from the stars.   (ll. 656–67).

Evidence of Browning's well known admiration of Shelley, these borrowings also underscore a fundamental contrast in temperament. Browning's still figure and tranquil viewer are radically unlike Shelley's frenzied maenad and excited call to deliverance. This combination of passivity and expectancy is distinctive and, since it recurs in Browning's rescue poems, worth pursuing.

DeVane mentions that Browning kept a print of Caravaggio's painting on his desk and calls attention to Browning's Perseus-like intervention into the life of Elizabeth Barrett.[2] The implication is that Browning enjoys the part of the savior, and as far as it goes, DeVane's hint is useful. Even a cursory glance through Browning's volumes indicates that Perseus has an extraordinary number of counterparts. A gallant horse and rider "save Aix from her fate" in "How they Brought the Good News" (l. 46), while a Breton sailor manages to "save the squadron" of twenty-two ships in "Hervé Riel" (l. 140). A woman takes grave chances in "The Italian in England," risking the Austrians' revenge "if once they find [she] saved their foe" (l. 70), while a goddess intervenes in "Artemis Prologizes" on behalf of a wronged votary. In "Count Gismond" a knight defends a lady who later prays "Christ God who savest men, save most / Of men Count Gismond who saved me!" (ll. 1–2). Browning's handling of these rescues, however, does not always or solely emphasize daring action. Artemis' monologue ends on a note of intense quiet as she awaits "the event" of Hippolutos' rebirth;[3] and Lady Gismond stresses her contented joy at the knight's sudden appearance:

> I never met
> His face before, but, at first view,
> I felt quite sure that God had set
> Himself to Satan; who would spend
> A minute's mistrust on the end?   (ll. 68–72)

> This glads me most, that I enjoyed
> 　　The heart of the joy, with my content
> In watching Gismond unalloyed
> 　　By any doubt of the event:
> God took that on him—I was bid
> Watch Gismond for my part: I did.　　　　(ll. 79–84).

The certitude of this "calumniated innocent" may seem exaggerated and unrealistic, but the relation between powerlessness and confidence is of special interest to Browning.[4] The lady's serenity on this occasion is akin to the tranquility that distinguishes the Andromeda passage. The maiden in the earlier poem "awaits the snake" but her admirer expects the arrival of "some god" to save her. Despite Andromeda's complete helplessness, the speaker knows her liberation is inevitable, "a thing / I doubt not nor fear for" (ll. 665–66). Such sure anticipation differs notably from the speaker's anxiety about himself and suggests that a fondness for heroes is not the only force at work in the passage. In Browning's poetry fascination with a helpless victim can be a species of wish-fulfillment; and displaced confidence, a potential convert's way of expressing his longing for change.

In Browning's mind, there is merit in certain kinds of defenselessness. Individuals with well-protected identities tend to be morally intransigent. The skill of the Duke in "My Last Duchess" and the mastery of Bishop Blougram—what George Eliot called his "self-complacent sense of supreme acuteness and . . . crushing force of worldly common sense"[5]—are spiritual liabilities. When such urbanity and lucidity are combined in "A Forgiveness," they produce a monster of self-control, a vengeful Spaniard who proceeds "to explain" that he refused for three years to look his wife in the face:

> 　　though daily, smile to smile,
> We stood before the public,—all the while
> Not once had I distinguished, in that face
> I paid observance to, the faintest trace
> Of feature more than requisite for eyes
> To do their duty by and recognize:
> So did I force mine to obey my will
> And pry no further. There exists such skill,—
> Those know who need it.　　　　(ll. 215–223).

Individuals must be less guarded than the Duke, Bishop, or Hidalgo to be capable of renovation. Only those less in control of their identities and language are susceptible to influence. The undefended self, whether enervated or innocently trusting, is, in Browning's view, the self that can be saved.

A brief comparison of Caravaggio's *Andromeda* with Guido Reni's *St. Sebastian*, another painting Browning is known to have admired, helps clarify Browning's interest in the imperiled and defenseless.[6] Both the martyr and the maiden gaze with dark eyes "earnest and still" while bound "naked and alone." The one will be saved physically and the other spiritually, but what the paintings have in common *visually* is the exposed vulnerability of their subjects. Incapable of exertions on their own behalf, these figures appeal because they are beyond resistance. Their helplessness is, of itself, a kind of innocence, and Browning's use of such figures suggests something more than a tacit identification with Perseus. The reference in *Pauline* is a way of indicating that the speaker's enervation has some advantages; his condition is promising. Pauline's poet thinks of the defenseless Andromeda because he, too, is an abject victim. Oppressed by doubt, apathy, and silence, he imagines the kind of assistance he personally requires. Unable to play his own Perseus, or to save himself from himself, he yearns to be rescued by some external force. He is ready, in other words, to be converted.

The degree of his helplessness is indicated by his reference to an earlier occasion when the "feeling rushed / That [he] was low indeed" (ll. 68–69) and he first told Pauline "all" (l. 71). She urged him to "look up and be what [he] had been (l. 74), but her exhortations had no effect and his confession proved a lament which brought no release. The significance of this episode is that confession does not automatically entail relief. Although attention can be turned inward, self-knowledge is elusive, and internal division persistent. The self can be in such disarray that renewal seems a thing hardly to be seized. Change, under these circumstances, can be imagined only as an inadvertent accomplishment, something wrought by an external agent. Relief must come, if at all, like a sudden rescue. Hence the significance of Andromeda; the security the speaker feels on her behalf is a projection of the security he would like to feel for himself. Through her he expresses the hope of passively achieved salvation.

Unfortunately, gods do not "come in thunder from the stars" to aid dispirited young men. The speaker's condition, moreover, is an interior one, and so the image of Andromeda yields to that of an aged man. A second passage describes the transformation of an individual rather than a situation, a conversion instead of a rescue. Browning is thinking of Edmund Kean when describing a

> wondrous mind,
> Yet sunk by error to men's sympathy,
> And in the wane of life.   (ll. 669–71).[7]

Browning saw Kean as Richard III and was struck by the vigor of the actor's performance and his apparent triumph over age and "decay." Pauline's poet identifies hypothetically with such a figure:

> and there shall come
> A time requiring youth's best energies;
> And lo, I fling age, sorrow, sickness off,
> And rise triumphant, triumph through decay.   (ll. 672–75).

The easy transition from Andromeda to Kean emphasizes the association of rescue and renovation. The maiden's passivity blends with the actor's debility, and the idea of release merges with that of self-transcendence. When the speaker admits that these changes are emblems of moral restoration, supplying "the chasm / 'Twixt what I am and all I fain would be" (ll. 676–77), his comment applies to their function throughout Browning's poetry. Tales of deliverance are often his way of broaching the subject of spiritual salvation. Imminent rescue is his symbol for immanent change, and what appear to be stories of release or flight are most often accounts of conversion. Rarely concerned with the rescuers themselves, unless they too need to be rescued, Browning has as his primary interest the change that takes place in the victim's soul.

In "The Flight of the Duchess" help comes in the person of "the oldest Gipsy then above ground" (l. 397). A very unpromising deliverer with "worn-out eyes, or rather eye-holes / Of no use now but to gather brine" (ll. 405–06), this hideous old woman offers not only a means of flight, but the challenge of restoration. As a young bride, the

Duchess has a vitality that communicates itself:

> She was active, stirring, all fire—
> Could not rest, could not tire—
> To a stone she might have given life!   (ll. 174–76).

But her husband has a passion for medieval charade, and his effort to revive "all usages thoroughly worn-out" (l. 116) reduces the Duchess' life to a depleting sham. Requiring that she "sit thus, stand thus, see and be seen" (l. 189), he seems not to notice that she is "pressed by fatigue" (l. 285) or to care that she "die[s] away the life between" (l. 191). So Browning allows the preternatural crone to come to the Duchess' aid. When the gypsy-Perseus offers a new way of life—"A real life," as Browning writes to Elizabeth, "not an unreal one like that with the Duke"[8]—the lady's acceptance is a sure conclusion. She will abandon the Duke and his historical games in order to recover her original self. Since Browning is more concerned with identities than escapes, he has his gypsy describe a soul-making life of joy and suffering. She promises the Duchess a series of trials that will prove her nature. Hers will be an ordeal of verification, a purging that is likened to

>   a jewel-finder's fierce assay
> Of the prize he dug from its mountain-tomb—
> Let once the vindicating ray
> Leap out amid the anxious gloom,
> And steel and fire have done their part.   (ll. 602–06).

The ferocity of "steel and fire," which might logically be used as a symbol of inflicted pain and oppression, represents the means of release. These purgings will be liberating.

The idea of assaying substances recurs in Browning's poetry and is often relevant to the process of "vindicating" or freeing the individual's true identity. The heroine of "In a Gondola" urges her lover to "loose" her spirit with sexual alchemy:

>   'Tis said, the Arab sage,
> In practising with gems, can loose
> Their subtle spirit in his cruce

    And leave but ashes: so, sweet mage,
    Leave them my ashes when thy use
    Sucks out my soul.   (ll. 31–36)

In "The Glove," Peter Ronsard approves a lady who tests the integrity
of her suitor's extravagant speeches. A "sensible experimentalist," in
one critic's phrase, she is represented as judge and chemist who "tried
in a crucible, / To what 'speeches like gold' were reducible" (ll.
111–112).[9] In similar fashion, Rabbi Ben Ezra approves of growing
old; he finds that life itself is purifying: "Leave the fire ashes, what
survives is gold" (l. 87). And Guido, giving the image its ultimate appli-
cation, speaks of death as the fiery release of "something changeless at
the heart of me / To know me by, some nucleus that's myself"
(XI. 2395). His accumulated sins are mere dross, removable "accre-
tions"; "Away with them— / You soon shall see the use of fire!"
(XI. 2396–97).

    The "fierce assay" of the soul's essence often takes the variant
form of torture; and suffering is conceived of as a formative oppor-
tunity, a means of achieving clarity. The Pope, in *The Ring and the
Book*, anticipates the formidable latter-day challenges which will make
the true man "stand out again, pale, resolute, / Prepared to die"
(X. 1862–63). The pontiff has Caponsacchi in mind, and the priest
himself conceives of his ethical struggle as a choice of martyrdoms. An
earthly woman claims his chaste passion, but his vocation requires
celibate and "pulseless" dedication (VI. 982); Pompilia asks him to
risk his life while the Church summons, "Come be dead with me!"
(VI. 1001). Bewildered by these rival demands, Caponsacchi cries out,
attempting to establish his allegiance:

    I am a priest! I see the function here;
    I thought the other way self-sacrifice:
    This is the true.   (VI. 1018–20).

These and countless other references to testing are not just a
mannerism. They are minor surfacings of Browning's major theme of
conversion. Expressions of his concern with authentic identity and
genuine roles, they affirm the possibility of harshly purifying trials.
    One of Browning's most subtly conceived ordeals of verification,

certainly his most urbane version of the soul's reduction, occurs in "Bishop Blougram's Apology." The "fierce assay" of the Duchess here finds a counterpart in the humiliation of Gigadibs. Blougram despises his auditor and plans to mortify him thoroughly: "You have had your turn and spoken your home truths; / The hand's mine now" (ll. 47–48). Even his preliminary epicurean directives—"try the cooler jug— / Put back the other, but don't jog the ice!" (ll. 132–33)—are peremptory attempts to disconcert the non-connoisseur. Unrelenting in attack, the bishop accuses Gigadibs of covetous insignificance. He summarizes the journalist's career as that of a trivial critic and Dickensian imitator and then patronizingly offers his compliments—"Success I recognize" (l. 954)—and his card. Directing his major attack at the disparity between Gigadibs' professed and actual ideals, Blougram remarks upon the social pretensions of the man who supposedly believes in being himself "plain and true" (l. 77). He even explains the hypocrisy of Gigadibs' free-thinking. If, as a disbeliever in revealed religion, the journalist fails to jettison the traditional moral code, "Then, friend, you seem as much a slave as I / A liar, conscious coward and hypocrite" (ll. 841–42). These remarks on Gigadibs' personal morality have an extraordinary result; they not only shame Gigadibs, but also rouse his "sudden healthy vehemence" (l. 1007). Blougram's contempt proves stimulating and his charge of insincerity alters the journalist's self-perception. No longer willing to be the creature the bishop describes, Gigadibs rejects his way of life, buys settler's tools and heads for Australia.[10] Blougram, wholly inadvertently, accomplishes a moral rescue; and the apology that prompts the flight of the journalist must be regarded as an authenticating assault.

The hostility which makes Blougram the least intentional of Browning's saviors does not, however, make him the most ironic. In Part IV of *Pippa Passes*, another churchman effects a rescue, but only after being roused by the very child he is tempted to victimize. The monsignor's intendant knows Pippa to be illegitimate, has used her in an extortion scheme, and now plans to corrupt and be rid of her; "at Rome the courtesans perish off every three years." (IV. 205–6). Some readers think it unpleasant of Browning to draw Pippa into the poem's sordid intrigue, but he is easily exonerated. This episode is a serious, if sensational, investigation of the varieties of power and powerlessness and the shifting relationship of the victim and the rescuer. As the Monsignor listens all too attentively to his intendant, Pippa's sweet voice suddenly awakens him to the horror of the man's proposal. Her innocence makes evil transparent and her vulnerability arouses the Monsignor's desire to use his strength, to be and to do good. Herein lies the significance of Pippa's involvement. The Monsignor's move to protect her is the direct result of the moral fervor she herself inspires. The meaning of such circularity is that the roles of Perseus and Andromeda are by no means mutually exclusive. A defenseless innocent may create her own savior, and the strong savior may be the morally needier of the two. Insofar as Pippa is both helpless and efficacious, she is an obvious ancestress of the suffering Pompilia. The victimized wife of *The Ring and the Book* must also rescue her rescuer. She too selects her own Perseus and endows him with the will to save her. When Caponsacchi confronts the judges, his chief purpose is to bear witness to the change Pompilia wrought in his soul.

The idea that the apparent saviors are themselves saved is susceptible to less ironic adaptations. The person who aids in another's renewal may, for example, accomplish his own soul's expansion; and the efforts of the innocent to help the despondent may bring blessings to both. An insight of this sort enables Browning, after several years' hiatus, to return to his unfinished "Saul."[11] The original nine stanzas concern Saul's spiritual restoration. Summoned by the priest, David finds his King in a state of life-denying enervation, alone and virtually crucified, "Both arms stretched out wide / On the great cross-support" of his tent (ll. 28–29). This identification with the suffering Christ is further emphasized by the duration of Saul's ordeal; he has been in "the black mid-tent's silence, a space of three days" (l. 7). And, since a resurrection of some sort is implied in David's wish for assurance that "the King liveth yet" (l. 5), it has been frequently and rightly urged that the "original incomplete version of 'Saul' (1845) left no doubt how the poem had to end."[12] A second strikingly anticipatory passage compares the king to a serpent awaiting annual "deliverance." Saul hangs immobile just as,

> caught in his pangs
> And waiting his change, the king-serpent all heavily hangs,
> Far away from his kind, in the pine, till deliverance come
> With the spring-time. (ll. 30–33).

This image derives its appropriateness from Biblical typology as well as natural history. In Numbers 21: 4–9, Moses raises a brazen serpent to heal the suffering Israelites; and in John's Gospel, this event becomes an image of salvation. When Nicodemus asks how a man "may be born again," the Savior himself draws the Old Testament analogy: "As Moses lifted up the serpent in the desert, even so must the Son of Man be lifted up, that those who believe in him may have life everlasting."[13] Thus the image of the serpent reinforces the suggestion of spiritual renewal and the imminence of Saul's rebirth.

The cause of the strife between "Saul and the Spirit" (1. 9) and the exact nature of the king's suffering are left unspecified. They are more terrible, perhaps, for being only intimated. What is clear is that this powerful and accomplished man has lost the will to live. Reality, as in Mill's phrase, has "ceased to charm" and, like Pauline's poet, Paracelsus, and even the Duchess, Saul has retreated into the isolation of his own despair.[14] To rescue Saul from this arid condition, David must stimulate and recover the King's own "sense of this world's life" (1. 51). David succeeds, not by philosophical abstractions—indeed, he is no more capable than Pippa of converting a man with coldly rational arguments—but by recounting the "wild joys of living" (1. 70). David's saving grace is sensuousness. Capable of generous sympathy, he surrenders himself to reality. The intimacy of his participation is borne out by the loving accuracy of his style. His song of the minutely seen and ecstatically heard is authoritative; the details which verify his commitment to life justify his role as counselor. David's song is compelling, not because his message is new, but because it is authentic. By sharing his intense experiences, he gives otherwise bland truths a force that is indisputable. This style also distinguishes his performance from that of his forerunner in *Pauline*. Where the earlier poem is vaguely inclusive and baldly generic, David's song is engagingly kinetic. The speaker in *Pauline* mentions "all the life of plants" (1. 716), but David feels how "the long grasses stifle the water within the stream's bed" (1. 39). The poet gazes "drowsily on bees" (1. 717) while David watches "the crickets elate / Till for boldness they fight one another" (ll. 43–44). The earlier speaker can "mount with the bird" (1. 720) or dive with the fish, but the latter knows the ways of the "quails on the cornland" (1. 42) and the "cool silver shock / Of the plunge in the pool's living waters" (ll. 71–72). David also sings of Saul's own feelings and puts the king in touch with the innermost forces of his being: his joy, his pride, and his tumultuously creative rage.

The energy of David's song, with its assertive rhythms, bounding anapests, and mouth-filling alliterations, endows reality with a new vibrancy. His precision and factuality counteract the formlessness of Saul's negation, and the entire episode dramatizes the lesson that "Fra Lippo Lippi" teaches about the value of shared perception:

> we're made so that we love
> First when we see them painted, things we have passed
> Perhaps a hundred times nor cared to see;
> And so they are better, painted—better to us,
> Which is the same thing. Art was given for that;
> God uses us to help each other so,
> Lending our minds out. (ll. 300–06).

The innocent David is just such a lender and his song of experience is effective. In the original poem, Saul's movement toward renewed confidence is signalled by a responsive groan; with this slight sound, he enters the company of Pippa's converts, the Duchess, and Gigadibs. He is one of the many characters Browning conceives of as morally rescued.

In the fuller version of the poem, David's task is considerably more complex. Having roused Saul from his state of retreat and denial, David faces a perplexing new difficulty. The king is suspended in a poignantly self-estranged state of indifference; like the soul in Arnold's "Stanzas from the Grande Chartreuse," he is caught "between two worlds, one dead, / The other powerless to be born."[15] David finds "death [is] past, life not come" (l. 119) and that Saul must be summoned not simply to life, but a new life appreciably more vital than the old. At this juncture, Browning solves what T. J. Collins aptly describes as a double problem; the poet finds "the artistic means necessary to render satisfactorily the religious consolation required to ease Saul's distressed spirit, and . . . the place of the singer in effecting the cure."[16] Collins' second point is of special interest, for in his crisis, David, like so many of Browning's characters, turns introspective. Powerlessness makes him self-referential, and frustrated longing makes him conscious of his ardor. Feelings of extreme but ineffective yearning alter his view of reality, and he suddenly knows the inadequacy of earthly joy:

> Could I help thee, my father, inventing a bliss
> I would add, to that life of the past, both the future and this;
> I would give thee new life altogether, as good, ages hence,
> As this moment,—had love but the warrant, love's heart to dispense!
> (ll. 233–36).

The poem turns on David's discovery of the world's relative insufficiency. In a letter to Julia Wedgwood, Browning offers an inadvertent gloss on this passage. While discussing the psychology of "the new birth," he observes that so long as "this life suffices, I don't see that another incentive to push on through its insufficiency, in the shape of a conceived possibility of a life beyond, is ever given us."[17] Indeed, the poem turns on the discovery of the "insufficiency" of life. It should be added, however, that the "incentive to push on" occurs in the context of self-scrutiny. David's sense of the world's limits is amplified by an awareness of the "love so full in his nature" (l. 266). This contrast is what prompts his flash of intuition. Unlike the young Sordello, who gives in to a solipsistic reverence for his soul's infinity, David is lead by his "fullness" to consider the possibility of divine love. His self-awareness flowers into prophecy and the desire to help Saul is transmuted into the promise of Christ's redemptive suffering. Because stanzas X to XIX concern David more directly than Saul, some readers feel that the poem is broken-backed and that "the relationship between the two figures becomes confusing."[18] But this is not really the case; the kind of substitution at work in *Sordello*—the economy whereby the narrator's experience intimates the hero's—functions here, too, with the effect that Saul's full renewal may be assumed.

The meaning of David's prophecy lies less in its messianic details than in the fact of his new sensibility. A rescuer who achieves transcendence, he is a savior whose experience is remarkably like that of the saved. The effort to change Saul's consciousness alters David's own and he, too, undergoes a crisis of awareness.[19] Once he conceives of God's perfect love, he becomes precociously attuned to the minutest evidence of nature's affirmation:

> I saw it die out in the day's tender birth;
> In the gathered intensity brought to the grey of the hills;

In the shuddering forests' held breath; in the sudden wind thrills;
In the startled wild beasts that bore off, each with eye sidling still
Though averted with wonder and dread; in the birds stiff and chill
That rose heavily, as I approached them, made stupid with awe:
E'en the serpent that slid away silent,—he felt the new Law.
The same stared in the white humid faces upturned by the flowers;
The same worked in the heart of the cedar, and moved the vine-bowers:
And the little brooks witnessing murmured, persistent and low,
With their obstinate, all but hushed voices—"E'en so! it is so!"
                                                            (ll. 325–35).

David's visionary prescience amounts to a reconfrontation of reality. And while Saul's may be the more nearly typical transformation, David's awakening to transcendence, insofar as it alters his relationship with the universe, falls within the conversion genre.

Even more important than the formal congruence of Saul's and David's episodes is their common psychology. Browning is able to finish his poem by considering the possibilities of self-knowledge. His concern with the varieties of intimacy leads to the discovery that conversion and expansion are both achieved through self-realization. If Saul can be saved by the experience of his soul's latent joy, then David can achieve vision as a reflex of his own love. His prophecy is an introspective attainment, the expression of a loving consciousness enraptured by its essential energies. Browning is not so blunt, however, as to allow David to articulate any such psychological theory. He lets the singer assume that his prophecy is a gift from God and has him pray,

       O Thou who didst grant me that day,
    And before it not seldom hast granted thy help to essay:
    . . . .
    Still be with me. . .
    . . . .
    Let me tell out my tale to its ending.   (ll. 191–99).

In his anthropomorphic piety, David describes the process of intuition as a divine elevation, "Just one lift of thy hand cleared that distance— God's throne from man's grave" (l. 198).

The theophanic character of this explanation is suitable for an Old Testament speaker, but it is consistent with Browning's practice in non-Biblical poems as well and serves a more basic purpose than that of characterization. Paracelsus' calling, for example, has both supernatural and psychological explanations; and the sudden eloquence that enables Sordello to triumph over silence is compared to a divinely accomplished rejuvenation:

> Come death
> Come life, he was fresh-sinewed every joint.
> Each bone new-marrowed as whom gods anoint.
>
> (V. 498–500).

In *Pippa Passes*, Ottima finds God's will unexpectedly wrought by the singer who prompts Sebald's conversion, and the lover of "By the Fireside" suspects that his moment of surrender is somehow the work of "powers at play" (1. 237). What is significant about Browning's use of the miraculous in these instances is the persistent comparison of the humanly interior with the divinely external. The character whose moral worth becomes suddenly apparent is as blessed as the recipient of a divine communication. Whether he learns of his shame as Sebald does, or his goal, as Paracelsus does, his self-confrontation has the effect of a sacred encounter. In similar fashion, the embarrassed artist or lover who sheds inhibition is thought of as receiving divine assistance; his moment of self-revelation seems a nearly supernatural event. Whether an individual's truth is suddenly perceptible to himself or another, its display, in Browning's view, is a crucial event. Whether the experience takes the form of discovery or disclosure, authentic self-knowledge is the highest achievement.

Moments of insight can be accounted for in purely psychological ways—such explanations are the motive of much of Browning's poetry—but by insisting so frequently on sacred causes and parallels, Browning elevates self-awareness to a grace. The moment of confrontation becomes an interior epiphany. Browning's practice anticipates James Joyce's, but the latter's definition of the word "epiphany," his theory of a "sudden spiritual manifestation" involving a "memorable phase of the mind itself," is applicable.[20] Browning knows as well as the modernist that the self is hardly ever all of itself at once. Human beings are "pent-up creatures" ("Dîs Aliter Visum" 1. 118) and the more controlled or confining an individual's identity, the more mysterious the unlived self. As alien as it is authentic, a pressing but awesome possibility, the other self seems a thing to be achieved only by incursion or miraculous expansion.

The result of Browning's attitude is not—as might at first be supposed—a profanely reductive poetry. The thrust of his art is not to demythologize, nor do his parallels and allusions imply that the sacred can be explained away psychologically. To get at the particular effect of Browning's countless theophanies, one should consider how many of his characters, even those who don't achieve epiphany, regard the world as divinely penetrable. Porphyria's lover sits all night challenging the God who "has not said a word!" (1. 60); Sludge claims to be a "seer of the supernatural / Everywhen, everyhow and everywhere" (1. 876). Even Caliban thinks that impudence elicits "His thunder" (1. 291). References to miraculously external intrusions are often specifically Biblical. The vision of Christ in *Christmas-Eve* is described in extravagant and blatantly New Testament detail. The narrator is summoned like Paul on the road to Damascus:

> As if in a thunder-peal
> Where one heard noise, and one saw flame,
> I only knew he named my name.   (ll. 1208–10).

and responds as does Peter at the Transfiguration:

>   let me build to thee
> Service-tabernacles three,
> Where, forever in thy presence,
> In ecstatic acquiescence,
> . . . .
> I may worship and remain!   (ll. 413–19).

Even Browning's settings seem to have theophanic expectations. A forest bathed in setting sunlight is described in *Pauline* as

>   quivering
> In light as some thing lieth half of life
> Before God's foot, waiting a wondrous change.   (ll. 183–5).

The landscapes often need release from an oppressive burden, and in

"Childe Roland" Nature herself expresses a desire for divine assistance:

> '. . . I cannot help my case:
> 'T is the Last Judgment's fire must cure this place,
> Calcine its clods and set my prisoners free.'   (ll. 64–66).

But nature is not always passive or helpless, and in *Christmas-Eve* the heavens take part in the drama of Christ's visitation. The clouds are "a-simmer with intense strain" (1. 203) and the sky is prescient "as if it knew / What, any moment, might look through" (ll. 195–6). Anticipation is heightened by the "moon's consummate apparition" (1. 378) and all is in readiness for something still more splendid:

> The black cloud-barricade was riven,
> Ruined beneath her feet, and driven
> Deep in the West; while, bare and breathless,
> North and South and East lay ready
> For a glorious thing.   (ll. 379–83).

A magnificent trio of moon bows then appears, and the premonition of the sky is fulfilled as Christ emerges from "the keystone of that arc" (1. 404). Buried in a long and unpopular poem, this beautiful lunar sequence is neither the first nor the last of its kind. Whether man awaits or nature participates, Browning's theophanies have a common quality. Whatever the context, the allusions themselves have an easy and unskeptical literalness of detail; and this unembarrassed quality is the best clue to Browning's attitude. Far from revealing a secularizing intention, these passages show a genuine fondness for Biblical spectacle and an intuitive acceptance of the idea of theophany. Browning would like to "See the Christ stand!" ("Saul," 1. 312). He would like to offer the greeting proposed in a sentimental but indicative anecdote. On several occasions, Browning is said to have repeated "with dramatic force" the comment by Charles Lamb concerning "Persons one would wish to have seen." After discussing philosophers and literary figures, he added, "There is one other Person—If Shakespeare was to come into the room, we should all rise up to meet him; but if that Person was to come into it, we should fall down and try to kiss the hem of his garment!"[21]

There is little modern evidence that this Person will appear, however, and the discrepancy between Browning's instinct for belief and the urgings of reason generate creative tension. The pressure of Browning's own doubt accounts in part for the persistence and variety of the theophanies in his poetry. As J. Hillis Miller notes in *The Disappearance of God*, Browning, like many of his contemporaries, longs for some evidence of the divine:

> Though Browning's poetry is so different in atmosphere from, say, Matthew Arnold's, though his world is a universe of plenitude rather than of poverty, he is like Arnold and like many other English writers of the nineteenth century in experiencing in his own way the withdrawal of God and the consequent impoverishment of man and his surroundings. Browning does not disbelieve in God, but he finds it impossible to approach him directly.[22]

Dismayed by the inaccessibility of an "orb-like o'ershrouded and inscrutable" deity (*Sordello*, III. 325), Browning bears, like his own Christians in *Christmas-Eve* and *Easter-Day*, "A Death in the Desert," and the Pope's monologue, the "burthen for late days" ("Death" l. 337). But it would be a mistake to suppose that Browning's theophanies serve only a nostalgic function or to imagine him as soothing a fundamentalist's desire with Biblically laced fantasies. Naive allusion is not his form of relief. Too sophisticated for such simple-hearted comfort, he works instead to solve the problem of divine remoteness by finding an alternative to miraculous intrusion. In his view, the essence of the theophanic event is not the spectacle, but the impact; not the visitation of God, but the revision of man. If God does not "come in thunder from the stars," this absence means only that self-confrontation is more subtly achieved. There must be an interior form of revelation and a non-miraculous route to the transcendent, and so Browning conceives of the human events and psychological impulses that set the individual before himself.

In "Saul" more emphatically than elsewhere, Browning defends the possibility of this interior and wholly human method of achievement. Subjective scrutiny may seem a very dubious way to discover either God's or the soul's truth, but through David, Browning validates the workings of authentic introspection. The singer's piety legitimizes his intuitive method, and his belief in God's intervention works positively to support Browning's theory of efficacious self-discovery. Similarly, when Browning is concerned with purely secular moments of truth, the religious analogy serves to affirm the spiritual importance of the event. Occasions of moral and aesthetic assessment are thus shown to have the potential of religious encounters. Far from using the psychological to diminish the sacred, Browning uses the sacred to validate the psychological. He assumes the value of the religious archetype and works to negotiate, not to deny, the distance between private epiphany and divine theophany.

The single source most appropriate for Browning's purposes is the Book of Revelation. Episodes such as the temporal millennium and Christ's final manifestation in time prove repeatedly stimulating, and Browning devotes an entire monologue to the apocalyptist himself. In "A Death in the Desert," the dying St. John addresses those early Christians who think Christ's return is imminent. Victims of a very literal belief, they grow increasingly bewildered each year the Second Coming remains unaccomplished. Some cling to fixed numbers and prepare to wait "Ten years longer (twelve, some compute)" (l. 678), while others grow frankly skeptical—"It is getting long ago: / Where is the promise of His coming" (ll. 176–77). Their alarm is intimately bound up with their belief in the Savior's divinity; and when they implore John to "Save our Christ!" (l. 330), he does so by correcting their time-bound expectations. Abandoning historical sequence altogether, he interprets his own vision, not as the description of a future era, but as an account of current reality. The last events have begun; Christ and the "antichrist" are "already in the world" (l. 158). This new teaching has the effect of internalizing the individual Christian's struggle; his task is not to remain faithful until the Divine return, but to see Christ manifest now:

> Is not God now i' the world His power first made?
> Is not His love at issue still with sin
> Visibly when a wrong is done on earth?   (ll. 211–13).

The awaited theophany is a matter of personal vision; the apocalypse is to be achieved not by endurance but by altered moral perception. Such a reinterpretation puts Browning's John in the mainstream of Biblical criticism; for as Meyer Abrams points out, there is a tendency among commentators "to internalize apocalypse by transferring the theater of events from outer earth and heaven to the spirit of the single believer."[23] Such a removal from macrocosm to microcosm is habitual in Browning and especially conspicuous in *Easter-Day*.

The speaker of this poem is a modern Christian who thinks he has seen Christ but ardently hopes he is deluded. The ambiguity is clumsy but purposeful, for it allows Browning to treat spectacular events—the end of the world and the Last Judgment—while directing attention to their psychological meanings. Robert Langbaum comments in *The Poetry of Experience* on the function of such strategy. His examples are from Keats but his analysis applies equally well to Browning.

> Keats, in trying in the "Ode to a Nightingale" to understand his mixed response to the bird's song, penetrates the song imaginatively . . . until, in the vision of the "magic casements," he achieves the insight which includes all the others, which, including both joy and pain and standing both inside and outside the world of sense and time, is finally adequate to his original perception. But the insight is itself an enigma and lasts only an instant—when the fading away of the bird's song breaks the union of subject and object, returning us to the world of ordinary perception and leaving us with the question:
>
> > Was it a vision, or a waking dream?
> > Fled is that music:—Do I wake or sleep?
>
> Does the poem, then, deny itself? What is left us in the end? The thing we are left with is the thing the observer is left with—a total movement of soul, a step forward in self-articulation. Like the observer in Keats' "La Belle Dame Sans Merci," we cannot be sure that the knight's dream of the beautiful lady is true or that his dream within a dream of the pale and vanquished knights is true. But we do know that his movement from dream to dream has revealed to him first beauty and then its terrible ambivalence, that something has happened to him. He can never be the same again—just as Coleridge's mariner can never be the same, whatever the truth of his narrative: and Lycius, in Keats' "Lamia," cannot live after losing the sight of Lamia's beauty, whether it be illusion or reality.[24]

Nor in Browning's poem can the narrator ever be the same. The more skeptical the reader's attitude towards the graphic but incredible theophanies of *Easter-Day*, the sooner he learns the true significance of the poem, namely, that the dream of apocalypse reforms the speaker.[25]

A projection of his inner state, the illusion of macrocosmic events precipitates microcosmic change.

The experience begins retrospectively; fearing that his religious commitment is inadequate, the narrator yearns to confess his deficiencies. As in *Pauline*, dissatisfied self-scrutiny leads naturally to thoughts of exposure and abrupt transformation. Longing and yet unable to shed his habitual ways, the speaker imagines unexpected disruptions of normalcy. He thinks how appropriately terrible it would be should the final consummation occur at Easter when the earth shows "all signs of meaning to pursue/ Her tasks as she was wont to do" (ll. 468-9). Then, by an obvious displacement, he imagines all creation subjected to the suspension he personally requires:

> —The skylark, taken by surprise
> As we ourselves, shall recognize
> Sudden the end. For suddenly
> It comes.   (ll. 470-73).

Reinforcing his speculations with a scrap from the gospels, the man who should but cannot relinquish his identity, dwells on the subversiveness of the event that catches the entire universe off guard:

> The dreadfulness must be
> In that; all warrants the belief—
> "At night it cometh like a thief."   (ll. 474-76).

The desire to be free of his identity is then cosmically realized. The earth's consummation takes place in a burst of Petrine fire that leaves

> exposed the utmost walls
> Of time, about to tumble in
> And end the world.   (ll. 544-46).

By one of the circular processes that Browning loves, this illusion of the end of time dispels the speaker's personal misconceptions. The fantasy of consummation effects a spiritual purging—"The intuition burned away / All darkness from my spirit too" (ll. 550-51)—and Revelation provides Browning yet another image for the fierce and authenticating "assay" of the self.

Less concerned with "earth's catastrophe" (*Sordello* IV. 686) than with the soul's ordeal, Browning uses eschatological violence to treat the destructive and fearsome aspect of renewal. Nor does he limit himself strictly to Revelation, but ranges freely among the books of the Old and New Testament. John's vision, after all, culminates a long tradition of Biblical violence, and there are countless instances of theophanic devastation available for Browning's purposes. He refers in passing to Sodom, Gomorrah, and the plagues, but also, in an important way, to the ancient Hebrew belief that one who looks on God will die. Confronted by Christ, the speaker of *Christmas-Eve* is "glutted with the glory" and feels his poor brain "burst asunder" (ll. 422–23):

> And out of it bodily there streamed
> The too-much glory, as it seemed,
> Passing from out me.   (ll. 425–27).

When Browning seeks images of destruction, nature, like Scripture, is a favorite source. Sometimes he uses terrestrial violence to reinforce divine, as in *Christmas-Eve* where the blast of God's glory is succeeded by the "cataract" of a "mighty fact" (ll. 441–2). But even without theophanic parallels, images of dangerous energy often suggest the catastrophic aspect of conversion. Festus, for example, conceives of Paracelsus' multiple crises as a series of creatively "convulsive throes" (V. 393) caused by a

> Sheet of winding subterraneous fire
> Which, pent and writhing, sends no less at last
> Huge islands up amid the simmering sea.   (V. 395–97).

In "Saul" the "one long shudder" (l. 115) which signals the king's affirmation is compared to the loosening of an avalanche: "fold on fold all at once it crowds thunderously down" (l. 108). The comparison is exaggerated, especially since the king emits only a groan and slightly shifts his stance, but the spectacular crashing of snow fields, like the rush of subterraneous fires, accurately suggests the terrible shock of spiritual reclamation. Even David's experience has violent consequences; his vision ended, hell seems to break loose. Motion implies emotion; eruption corresponds to rapture; and all nature partakes in his amazed awareness:

> The whole earth was awakened, hell loosed with her crews;
> And the stars of night beat with emotion, and tingled and shot
> Out in fire the strong pain of pent knowledge.   (ll. 317–19).

Spontaneous and intimidating, such disruptions in nature signify the importance of the interior event. To discover a grave truth, to shed an identity, or to transcend oneself is a psychically convulsive event.

In *Easter-Day* the speaker's dream of violent disillusionment is prelude to a confrontation with Christ as Judge. Unlike the loving savior anticipated in "Saul," Christ in this capacity is as intimidating as he is appealing. Possessed of complete knowledge of man's innermost being, he is the symbol of absolute self-awareness. Facing him, the dreamer feels fully exposed and does not even wait for the divine verdict. In a flash of moral recognition, he knows himself damned, "there, stood I, found and fixed, I knew" (l. 552). Moncure Conway, in a foolish and rather well-known remark, once accused Browning of hating "to give up anything scenic, even a day of judgment."[26] By implying that vividness is a major concern, Conway misses the point. The doomsday scenario appeals to Browning as an externalization of the moment of assessment. It is a dramatic projection of the confessional process. Nor is the connection between judgment and introspection always luridly handled. In *The Ring and the Book* Caponsacchi urges his judges to abandon their worldly cynicism for unskeptical wisdom. Drawing an analogy between their corrected vision and similar alterations to be accomplished at time's end, he warns simply, "Thus will it be with us when the books ope / And we stand at the bar on judgment-day" (VI. 145–46). In keeping, too, with Browning's association of spiritual reformation and eschatological violence, Caponsacchi identifies temporarily with the doomster who transcribes prophecies in some "cloister's chronicle" (VI. 219). The priest promises to remain as calm "as monk that croons" over texts that foretell "battle, earthquake, famine, plague" (VI. 216–17). The implication is clear; the change Caponsacchi hopes to accomplish amounts to a kind of de-construction. The judges, as individuals and as institutional officials, must cast off their ethical misconceptions.

Erring characters in Browning's poetry, whether they are seven-teenth century Italian judges or nineteenth century Englishmen, discover, if they confront themselves honestly, that their lives are the consequence of unexamined but deliberate decisions. They can, if they are courageous, transform themselves by acknowledging their faulty moral choices. Thus at the climax of *Easter-Day*, the speaker acknowledges before Christ that he is guilty of "choosing the world":

> The choice was made;
> And naked and disguiseless stayed,
> And unevadable, the fact.   (ll. 553–55).

With these few lines, the poem comes full circle, for this declaration resolves the query that prompted the entire dream. Examining the condition of his faith on Easter eve, the speaker originally wondered:

> How were my case, now, did I fall
> Dead here, this minute—should I lie
> Faithful or faithless?   (ll. 396–98).

Both the question and its reply recall numerous similar instances in which Browning's speakers confront themselves or one another with momentous spiritual choices. Even the rhetorical pattern is familiar. Browning is fond of reducing his characters' options and phrasing their challenges in neat dichotomies. Blougram, for example, proposes to the skeptical Gigadibs the same alternatives he has faced; " 'What think ye of Christ, friend?' when all's done and said, / Like you this Christianity or not?" (ll. 626–27). In *Christmas-Eve* the narrator examines his belief in Christ's nature by asking:

> The goodness,—how did he acquire it?
> Was it self-gained, did God inspire it?
> Choose which.   (ll. 950–52).

The question implies an obligation to select the one "best way of worship" (l. 1171). The speaker eventually reaches his decision with the words "I choose here!" (l. 1341). Repeatedly in Browning's poetry, "A man's choice . . . / Bears upon life, determines its whole course" ("Blougram," ll. 221–9); and while the issue is often religious, the specific questions are not always abstrusely theological. The narrator of "A Grammarian's Funeral" interprets his master's life as an ascetic's affirmation of the challenge "Wilt thou trust death or not?" (l. 111). Fra Lippo Lippi explains the disparity between his own and the Prior's views of the world with an eccentric metaphor and a burst of choices:

> The old mill-horse, out at grass
> After hard years, throws up his stiff heels so,
> Although the miller does not preach to him
> The only good of grass is to make chaff.
> What would men have? Do they like grass or no—
> May they or mayn't they? all I want's the thing
> Settled for ever one way.   (ll. 254–60).

Referring the matter finally to his auditors, Lippo describes the world with vigor and asks the soldiers to examine their responses; "Do you feel thankful, ay or no" (l. 286). Even Browning's lovers pressure themselves with baldly worded questions: "Heart, shall we live or die?" ("A Lovers' Quarrel," l. 145).

The clarity of such formulations appeals to Browning and under-scores his interest in the process of self-realization. The making of choices is a form of assertion, and the assessment of a choice can be a moral awakening. Browning is aware that an authentic choice is just a beginning, but he uses the moment of decision as synecdoche for the whole process of discovery and commitment. He imagines the soul, bolstered by the sense of urgency, shaking off the burden of its indeterminacy and bravely declaring itself "for ever one way." Even his moral cowards are aware of the awful significance of such occasions. They console themselves for their wasted and empty lives by fancying that they marched at least once to the "dangerous edge of things" ("Blougram," l. 395). The illusion of confronting the brink bestows a spurious aura of volition upon their subsequent with-drawals; and when the aura fades, they refresh it by rehearsing their supposed choices. The moribund and timid painter of "Pictor Ignotus" is one of these self-deceivers. Citing the "pettiness" of buyers as one cause of his aesthetic retreat, he soothes himself with the boast "I chose my portion" (l. 57). Andrea del Sarto is also an illusionist and a master of marital charade. His monologue has several elaborate purposes, one of which is to reach the amazing conclusion, ". . .there's still Lucrezia,—as I choose." (l. 266).

In *Easter-Day*, the speaker understands that his choice is reprehensible. Compelled by the dream to reverse his commitment, he finds that the illusion of Judgment has lasting consequences. In this poem then, as in "A Death in the Desert," apocalypse is a microcosmic event. Browning's internalization of Biblical episodes, moreover, is so habitual and his adaptation of Revelation so conspicuous that the critic may perform a similar act and borrow the term "apocalypse." The word is currently enjoying a vogue that makes further use undesirable and yet, in Browning's case, it is singularly appropriate. With only a slight adjustment of its authentic scriptural meaning, "apocalypse" can designate Browning's favorite kinds of crises. Like the word "epiphany," it suggests confrontation and spiritual discovery. Since John's vision concerns Christ's final manifestation in time, the term may be said to convey the same general idea. Both suggest the intersection of temporal and spiritual forces and the clash of worldly and transcendent values. The peculiar suitability of "apocalypse," however, lies in the greater richness of its connotations. Among the episodes in Revelation, besides the Second Coming, earth's dissolution and the Last Judgment, is the re-creation of heaven and earth. John writes:

> I saw a new heaven and a new earth: for the first heaven and the first earth were passed away; and there was no more sea. (Rev. 21:1)

> And he that sat upon the throne said, Behold I make all things new. (Rev. 21:5)

This event, like the others, can be interpreted with respect to man's inner life and is traditionally regarded as a type of rebirth. Thus the meaning of "apocalypse" comprises not only confrontation, destruction, and exposure, but reformation and renewal. Such exegesis underlies Browning's own use of Revelation and summarizes fairly comprehensively the major themes of his art. Each character who scrutinizes his soul conducts a potentially renovating exercise; each who is rejuvenated is in some way destroyed and made new. The goal Browning conceives for all of his victims and many of his saviors may be thought of as a personal apocalypse.

The possibility of renovating confrontation so fascinates Browning that even legal papers are susceptible to apocalyptic interpretation. Belief in man's potential for change influences his reading and permits him to find a tale of the soul's recreation in the diffuse trial documents of the *Old Yellow Book*.[27] To Browning's mind, the encounters of the priest and wife are occasions of self-realization and the rescue attempt is proof of Caponsacchi's moral awakening. So struck is Browning by the change he perceives in Caponsacchi that he makes the conversion of the "priest, coxcomb, fribble and fool" (VI. 98) the central episode of *The Ring and the Book*. The surrogate narrator of the introduction revels in the historicity of the poem:

> Do you see this square old yellow Book I toss
> I' the air, and catch again, and twirl about
> By the crumpled vellum covers,—pure crude fact
> Secreted from man's life when hearts beat hard,
> And brains, high-blooded, ticked two centuries since?
> Examine it yourselves?   (I. 33–38).

But for all this exultation over the facts of the story, Browning is as much stimulated by a hiatus in the narrative as by its details. He seizes on a two-day period unaccounted for in the source; the depositions indicate a delay—from the time of Caponsacchi's promise to aid Pompilia until their actual flight—but do not suggest how the priest spends this time.[28] Browning welcomes the lack of "pure crude fact." He not only supplies his own account of the climax of Caponsacchi's conversion, he makes it the core of the priest's monologue. Such amplification may well explain Browning's reluctance to publish the *Old Yellow Book* in the 1880s. When Furnivall makes the suggestion, Browning writes:

> I supposed, when the matter was mooted two years ago, that all wanted was to place a thing, absolutely *unique* of its kind, out of the possibility of loss or destruction—by fire, ignorance or whatever might be the accident,—a copy to be laid up in the archives of your Society, while the original was deposited at Balliol. I never thought of any measure which would,—so to speak—pull up my tree and exhibit the roots to the "Public"—whose sagacity I have had a half-a-century's experience of.

Before setting to work on the Poem, I examined the "Book" thoroughly; and the result is all that I wish my readers to be acquainted with. . . .[29]

The "result" in Caponsacchi's monologue is a completely unverifiable two-day apocalypse. To affirm the change Caponsacchi can hardly understand, Browning fills his monologue with references to the Book of Revelation.[30] Biblical allusions are appropriate for a cleric; Caponsacchi even exclaims "I am a priest,—talk of what I have learned" (VI. 60) But the peculiar fitness of Caponsacchi's references has less to do with his priesthood than with the "revelation of Pompilia" (VI. 1865). Lines 937–1084 describe the painful, exhilarating, and utterly non-rational climax of this innocent woman's influence. She reforms Caponsacchi spiritually, and he speaks of the experience in terms of destruction and renovation. Hers is a moral force that abolishes the interiorized "weight o' the world" and establishes a new order:

> It was the first Spring.
> By the invasion I lay passive to,
> In rushed new things, the old were rapt away;
> Alike abolished—the imprisonment
> Of the outside air, the inside weight o' the world
> That pulled me down.   (VI. 946–51).

> Into another state, under new rule
> I knew myself was passing swift and sure.   (VI. 964–65).

He reinforces his convert's testimony with a reference to the Lamb's train of virgin followers. The scriptural source reads:

> And I looked, and, lo, a Lamb stood on the mount Sion, and with him an hundred forty and four thousand, having his Father's name written in their foreheads.   (Rev. 14:1.)

> These are they which were not defiled with women; for they are virgins.   (Rev. 14:4.)

These virgins are traditionally identified with the undefiled Christians raised in triumph on the last day. Caponsacchi describes himself, in the throes of moral transformation, as a member of this rising band:

> The initiatory pang approached,
> Felicitous annoy, as bitter-sweet
> As when the virgin-band, the victors chaste,
> Feel at the end the earthly garments drop,
> And rise with something of a rosy shame
> Into immortal nakedness: so I
> Lay, and let come the proper throe would thrill
> Into the ecstasy and outthrob pain.   (VI. 966–73).

This passage is extraordinarily dense even for Browning. Of all the occasions of conversion and awakening scattered throughout his poetry, only this suggests both exposure and orgasm. The priest who can no longer endure the self-caricature of his worldly churchman's identity feels this "earthly garment" drop. Like a true convert he welcomes definitive "nakedness." Innocently embarrassed with a "rosy shame," he is thrilled by the undisguised emergence of his essential self. Instead of the rushing and terrible release Sebald feels, Caponsacchi experiences a passive and almost sexual ecstasy as he relinquishes his identity and surrenders to a newly conscious, authentic self.

Although this personal transformation is complete, sure, and irrevocable, Caponsacchi does *not* move immediately to help Pompilia. His promise to take her to Rome prompts the convert's first crisis of conscience. Finding himself "i' the grey of dawn . . . / Facing the pillared front" of his church (VI. 974–75), he confronts for the first time the true meaning of priesthood and concludes, mistakenly, that his vocation precludes flight with a lady. Despite the power and vividness of this episode, it is frequently slighted by critics. E. D. H. Johnson, for example, ignores it altogether when he writes that, after their first interview,

> the confederacy of Pompilia and Caponsacchi against the world is a foregone conclusion. In her time of need Caponsacchi without a moment's hesitation brushes aside the proprieties, unmindful that his conduct in arranging Pompilia's escape is on the face of it a betrayal of his priestly duties.[31]

And Isobel Armstrong, who writes perceptively of Caponsacchi's tendency to "describe his experiences in terms of sudden, apocalyptic, revelatory events," seems not to notice the Biblical language used in this episode.[32] The challenge presented by the Church, a challenge Caponsacchi projects in a kind of dream vision, is articulated in apocalyptic terms. In Revelation 21:9–10, the establishment of the new order is signaled by the marriage of the Lamb to his bride, the heavenly city:

> and [he] talked with me, saying, Come hither, I will shew thee the bride, the Lamb's wife. And he carried me away in the spirit to a great and high mountain, and shewed me that great city, the holy Jerusalem, descending out of heaven from God, . . .

By an easy extension of this marriage metaphor, Caponsacchi identifies himself as the groom and his church as the spouse:

> My church: it seemed to say for the first time
> "But am not I the Bride, the mystic love
> O' the Lamb, who took thy plighted troth, my priest. . . ?"
> (VI. 976–78).

The notion of mystical betrothal lends itself to sensual treatment; Caponsacchi's usage, however, is conspicuously unerotic. His church is a passionless and threatening bride who offers to "fold thy warm heart on my heart of stone / And freeze thee" (VI. 979–80). Frigid though she is, she accuses him of infidelity and urges him *not* to aid Pompilia. To help a "fleshly woman" (VI. 981) would be a betrayal of his priestly troth; "let the free / Bestow their life-blood" (VI. 981–82). Because Caponsacchi desires to enact his priestly ideals and to live in a way befitting his new identity, he submits to the "authoritative word" of his ecclesiastical spouse:

> I obeyed. Obedience was too strange,—
> This new thing that had been struck into me
> By the look o' the lady, —to dare disobey
> The first authoritative word. 'T was God's.   (VI. 1010–13).

Motivated by Pompilia herself—she has prompted "this new thing," his desire to be an obedient priest—Caponsacchi paradoxically abandons her. So strong is his wish to help her that it becomes the first sacrifice on the altar of his new-found asceticism.[33] Later when the Pope criticizes those who fail Pompilia, he uses a variation of Caponsacchi's own marriage image. Condemning the clergy as the unfaithful spouse who "betrays the Bridegroom here" (X. 1491), he approves service to Pompilia as a form of fidelity. Caponsacchi, however, has no such Papal support at the time of his decision, and Browning's purpose in allowing him to desert Pompilia involves more than a love of irony. Caponsacchi's misconception of his priestly role is a source of self-division, a moral obstacle to be surmounted without authoritative assistance. Because flight with Pompilia is officially unwarrantable, Caponsacchi's decision must be courageously "self-authorized" (VI. 920). His triumph, as Browning sees it, is his independent discovery that Pompilia's rescue is "consistent with [his] priesthood" (VI. 139). The attempt to save her is the convert's form of self-assertion. Every mile towards Rome confirms his new identity.[34]

When Caponsacchi discusses the flight, he again turns to Revelation. He recalls the confidence he felt and phrases his expectation in terms of final resurrection. As serene as Gismond's lady or Pauline's poet, throughout their ride he is sure of safe arrival and a new life for Pompilia:

> I said to myself—"I have caught it, I conceive
> The mind o' the mystery: 't is the way they wake
> And wait, two martyrs somewhere in a tomb
> Each by each as their blessing was to die,
> Some signal they are promised and expect,—
> When to arise before the trumpet scares:
> So through the whole course of the world they wait
> The last day, but so fearless and so safe!"   (VI. 1183–90).

This mood prevails during the first trial and Pompilia's subsequent confinement. As long as she is out of Guido's reach, Caponsacchi considers her safe and regards himself as her effective rescuer; he tells the judges "I thought I had saved her" (VI. 1591). But Caponsacchi cannot prevent Guido's final act of butchery; the dragon-husband slays Andromeda after all and brutally nullifies the priest's role as Perseus. The news of the stabbing is the sudden "extremity" (VI. 28) which motivates Caponsacchi's monologue. Bereft of Pompilia and cheated of his great self-verifying act, the unhappy priest—"O great, just, good God! Miserable me!" (VI. 2105)—feels a dire need to reconstruct his identity. Pained and confused, he plunges, like other Browning confessants, into vehement, erratic, and honest self-scrutiny. His purpose is re-evaluation, and he tells the judges "I need that you should know my truth" (VI. 342). He needs, specifically, to bear witness to the change Pompilia wrought in him. The news that forces him to re-examine his role necessarily directs his attention to her; as he testifies to her remarkable power, it becomes clear that she is the true savior in this story. Her influence awakens him to his spiritual inadequacy; her helplessness provides the chance to verify his conversion. She is, in short, the true Perseus here. She effects a moral rescue even Guido cannot nullify.

Caponsacchi's is by no means the last monologue in *The Ring and the Book*, and for an explicit assessment of the priest's apocalypse one may look to the Pope's meditation. Examining the papers related to the murder, the pontiff remarks how abysmally "the Christians here deport them" (X. 1452). Lamenting the behavior of Guido and those who "with all the aid of Christ succumb" (X. 1900), he envisions still worse times to come, an "antimasque" comparable to the era of the Biblical antichrist:

> Do not we end, the century and I?
> The impatient antimasque treads close on kibe
> O' the very masque's self it will mock,—on me
> Last lingering personage, the impatient mime
> Pushes already.   (X. 1903–07).

The Pope does not, however, foresee a subsequent age of Christian triumph or anything so literal as Christ's thousand-year reign promised in Revelation 20:4. Instead, he conflates Biblical chronology and internalizes the millennial episode. There will not be any re-creation of the temporal epoch, but rather of the individual soul. The "gloriously-decisive change" (X. 1615) will, like Caponsacchi's, be a private and interior achievement, an accomplishment in spite of the world's evil. The Pope approves Caponsacchi's "brave starry birth" (X. 1154) and allows this example to assuage his grief about the "mass of men whose very souls even now / Seem to need re-creating" (X. 1893–94). Recognizing Caponsacchi's integrity and his pain, the

Pope advises the convert to "Deserve the initiatory spasm, once more / Work, be unhappy but bear life, my son!" (X. 1211–12).

The Ring and the Book is Browning's testament of faith in the possibility of genuine self-realization. His is not a naive confidence; he freely admits that Pompilia and Caponsacchi are miraculous people. And his poem amply, even overwhelmingly, demonstrates how society militates against miracles and how the world requires duplicity and cynicism. Browning is well aware of the pressures which corrupt an individual's authentic nature. Pompilia expresses Browning's own attitude when she speaks of Guido's efforts "to make me and my friend unself ourselves, / Be other man and woman than we were" (VII. 707–08). Nonetheless, *The Old Yellow Book* seems to Browning to provide historical evidence of one soul's re-creation. Caponsacchi's renovation seems to prove, in a revision of Pompilia's phrase, that a man can self himself. Caponsacchi's tale confirms Browning's sense of man as a potential convert and vindicates all his poems of deliverance and transformation. Degraded by his status as a "courtly spiritual cupid," Caponsacchi is as victimized by his role as Saul is by his enervation or the Duchess by her husband's charades. As susceptible to innocence as Sebald or Pippa's Monsignor, he lies fortunately "passive" to Pompilia's moral "invasion" (VI. 947). He responds to her as self-referentially as David to Saul and attempts her rescue because he, like the actor in *Pauline*, has achieved self-transcendence. And at the shock of her murder he is moved, like all Browning's confessants, to lay bare his soul. The critic need not worry that Browning may have misunderstood his sources or that Caponsacchi's apocalypse is non-historical. The very possibility of a corrected or alternative reading of the *Old Yellow Book* underscores the idiosyncrasy of Browning's interpretation. He believes in man's urge to be honestly exposed and in his desire to be remade. He believes in the moral force of innocence and the renovating power of self-confrontation. To recognize these beliefs is to discover the motive and injunction behind Browning's poetry.

3

"No Bar Stayed Me":
The Confession Manqué

Though it may seem strange that the creator of David and Capon-sacchi should also give the world Andrea and Sludge, Browning is, nonetheless, as well known for his manipulative monologists as for his honest ones. His belief in the possibility of genuine introspection in no way diverts his attention from humanity's capacity for guile. On the contrary, a scrupulous moral subtlety compels him to dramatize the mechanisms of fraudulent self-consciousness. His sense of man's longing for epiphany requires him to consider the anxieties which work to subvert it. To think of man as a potential convert, susceptible to shame and willing to change, Browning must also take notice of the general tendency for moral resistance. Committed by his own honesty to assess man's obstinacy, Browning finds the issue unexpectedly fascinating. The study of intransigence and perceptual failure leads him into a whole new genre. Considering lost occasions does more for the poet than clarify the dynamics of those that save; it makes him curious about the psychology of self-delusion. With skilled sympathy, he contemplates the inhibitions which keep men ignorant of them-selves, and makes poetry of their impediments. Richard Howard allows Browning to confess this fascination in the dramatic monologue "November, 1889." The poet proclaims to his son, in memorably succinct fashion, "I am not interested in art. / I am interested in the obstacles / to art."[1]

This eagerness to consider obstacles is one of the distinctive qualities of Browning's poetry, the source of multeity amid unity. His characters share the goal of self-knowledge, but each confronts his own special barriers. Each has private vulnerabilities which contribute to the rich particularity of Browning's art. The unknown painter wants consolation for his anonymity, but Blougram seeks to dominate his critic. The Bishop of St. Praxed's fears mortality, while Johannes Agricola dreads corruption, and Karshish, his own irrationality. So common is it for Browning's characters to be morally or aesthetically inhibited that their occasional assertions to the contrary, as in "I'm my own master, paint now as I please" ("Fra Lippo Lippi," l. 226), should be met with skepticism. The character who feels completely unhampered is probably self-deceived and his lack of frustration is, in itself, an indication that something is wrong. When, for example, the confined Agricola plots a journey through the "roof" of night, the deluded literalness of his reverse epiphany is distressing:

> No suns and moons though e're so bright
>   Avail to stop me; splendour-proof
>   I keep the broods of stars aloof.   (ll. 3–5).

But the audacity of his sense of election, his belief in the smoothly effectual "progress of the elect," is a more alarming sign of spiritual aberration. In the sane and natural order of experience, Agricola ought to feel thwarted.

The fears of Browning's characters often commit them to strategic falsifications. Rather than face terrifying truths, they resort to subterfuge and evasion. Some of the most introspective monologists resist the revelations they seem to seek. Adept at preventing their epiphanies, they can distort the past to justify the present, cling to old habits at the moment of illumination, and project their personal limitations onto all they contemplate. Obtuse confessants and disingenuous apologists, masters of blunted self-criticism and transferred blame, they have numerous ways of forestalling the discovery of the soul's true worth. And to accommodate their ruminations, Browning develops a new mode, one that might be called the confession manqué.

"Pictor Ignotus" is an early example of this new genre. Personal anxiety blocks the painter's self-scrutiny, while cowardice distorts his recollections. Instead of admitting his aesthetic inadequacy, he comforts himself and works to sustain his illusions. His monologue opens with the memorable boast that he "could have" produced works of nearly cosmic splendor:

> I could have painted pictures like that youth's
>   Ye praise so. How my soul springs up! No bar
> Stayed me—ah, thought which saddens while it soothes!
>   —Never did fate forbid me, star by star,
> To outburst upon your night with all my gift
> Of fires from God.   (ll. 1–7).

The claim that he would have "sunk / To the centre, of an instant" (ll. 9–10) implies the absence of any restraint which might preclude achievement. But his inherently plausible assertion, "No bar / Stayed me" (ll. 2–3), is suspect, and his monologue, like Agricola's, supplies ample evidence of the obstacles he tries to deny.[2]

The painter's chief difficulty is his obtrusive and timid self-regard. He supposes, like the young Sordello, that the purpose of art is to glorify the artist, and he longs for the crowd's adulation. Imagining the arrival of one of his *works* in some "glad aspiring little burgh" (l. 30), he speaks confusedly of how its admirers "greet / *My* face . . . lie learning at *my* feet!" (ll. 33–35, italics mine). Continuing in this peculiarly literal vein, he associates his personal fate with that of his picture and fancies himself posthumously loitering, savoring the world's esteem:

> Oh, thus to live, I and my picture, linked
> With love about, and praise, till life should end,
>   And then not go to heaven, but linger here,
> Here on my earth, earth's every man my friend.   (ll. 36–39).

The inability to distinguish between himself and his canvas is symptomatic, and the painter's appropriation of his picture's praise is not the strongly egotistical act it might at first seem. Browning supplies a subtle indication of the painter's mentality in his slightly stilted syntax. The faint awkwardness of "linked / With love about, and praise" and the eked-out repetitiveness of "not go to heaven, but linger here, / Here on my earth, earth's every man my friend" betray hesitant carefulness. The significant feature of this fantasy is its cautiousness, the way the unknown painter asserts himself—invisibly. He plans to behave in his triumph like one of the "wronged" painters of "Old Pictures in Florence":

> Their ghosts still stand, as I said before,
>   Watching each fresco flaked and rasped,
> Blocked up, knocked out, or whitewashed o'er:
>   —No getting again what the church has grasped!
> The works on the wall must take their chance.   (ll. 185–89).

The ghostliness of the painter's attendance upon an unpainted master-piece suggests that a fear of exposure undermines his hunger for public notice. Felt in life as well as fantasy, this dread is the cause of his professional retreat. Paralyzed with self-concern, he is afraid of his art and refuses to commit himself to a distinctive style.

The most noteworthy aspect of "Pictor Ignotus" is that it deals with present as well as past inhibitions. Old anxieties operate with new effect and the painter's ambiguous self-concern distorts the confessional process. The drama of the monologue derives from his efforts to maintain rather than dispel certain gratifying illusions. Remembering how he nursed an aesthetic dream, he asserts that "a voice changed it!" (I. 41). The precise nature of this crisis is not recounted, but a powerful analogy is employed:

> sights
> Have scared me, like the revels through a door
> Of some strange house of idols at its rites!   (ll. 41–43).

Carnality then escalates to savagery in lines that suggest the rape of a cringing nun. In the same breath the painter speaks of the callousness of those who traffic in art, and here the reader resists. Bourgeois insult can be compared to sexual assault, but the painter's image is too sadistic to apply meaningfully to those who "buy and sell" (l. 50) pictures. The result of intense dread rather than past fact, this exaggerated memory of his artistic chastening has less to do with the vulgarity of merchants and critics than with the painter's fears about himself. Possessed of only the shakiest sense of his own being, he cannot endure scrutiny. These lines indicate, too, that his opening boast is simply a species of wish-fulfillment; the arch traditionalist who thinks himself capable of stellar revelation is incapacitated by the fear of exposure. His entire meditation attempts to justify a failure it does not fully acknowledge, his terrified refusal to "all-express" ("One Word More," l. 111) himself.

The painter's experience of the world's hostility strikes him, now as then, with the force of an apparent epiphany. It seems to him to legitimize both his rejection of artistic fame and his withdrawal from the market place. It enables him to view his past with muted pride and to assume the stature which Browning habitually ascribes to those who make some "terrible choice" (*The Ring and The Book*, X. 1238) in life. The memory of this event, however falsified, permits the painter to claim "I chose my portion" (l. 57). The gratification he feels making this assertion derives from the connotation of the verb "choose." By implying the existence of genuine options, it bolsters the illusion that the painter "could have" selected another portion in life. The less flattering truth, of course, is that his sight of the buyers and critics only approximated an epiphany. Their "cold faces" supplied an excuse to abandon a frightening artistic mode, one that required the aggressive projection of the self. In his current need, the painter seizes upon the myth of unfulfilled promise and pretends to a talent greater than that he exhibits to the world. Supposing, as do all Browning's silent poets, that a rich potentiality hoards itself in his soul, he fondly believes that unexerted powers remain unexhausted as well. His monologue is a protective fiction, a distorted narrative that perpetuates his original failure. By focusing his life around a falsified crisis, he is able to identify himself in terms of hypothetical greatness. He need never ask why he fears critical exposure. He can permanently avoid artistic risks and continue to deny his limitations.

The result of such self-deception is frightful, for it commits the painter to a life of tedious and unredeeming strategy. The artist who cannot, in fantasy, maintain sufficient distance between himself and his art protects his identity, in practice, by establishing too much distance. He resorts to the old idiom, the "way of safe copying precedents."[3] Glad of sanctioned limits, he welcomes the monotony of the authorized series because it allows him to distinguish between his talent and his productions. Pictures that do not exercise him cannot be used to measure his soul, and his masterworks remain safely unexecuted. He can leave the world as does Waring, with "great works undone" ("Waring," l. 27). It is deeply ironic that the man who dreams of paintings that encircle him with love uses his frescoes to form an enclosing barrier. He keeps them from the world, hidden in "the endless cloisters and eternal aisles" (l. 59), but they also keep the world from him. Such strategy is its own punishment and proves ultimately more damaging than outright failure. He never knows the pain that is exhilarating or the frustration that piques desire. And so, despite his willed distance, a subtle identification between artist and artifact does exist. His acceptance of the old forms represents the death of artistic desire. The lines in which he croons elegiacally over his moldering pictures might well be read on behalf of his own soul. They die together.

The monologue concludes with a rhetorical question about the worthlessness of popular approval. In a final small-minded maneuver, the painter addresses the rival youth "men praise so" and asks, "holds their praise its worth?" (l. 70). It is fitting that a poem of non-discovery should end as it began, with an expression of resentment over another's success. Rhetorical circularity reinforces the impression of the speaker's resistance. Defensiveness makes him denigrating, and a younger man's triumph only stimulates his powers of self-deception.

The connection between the ungenerous and the non-genuine in man's nature is borne out in several of Browning's poems, most strikingly in "The Bishop Orders his Tomb." The Bishop of St. Praxed's is as begrudging towards his rival as the unknown painter and more protractedly resistant to truth. His lifelong resentment of "Old Gandolf" increases with the approach of death and subverts what ought to be a final confession. Because the Bishop's desire to outdo his predecessor ought to give way to more appropriate sentiments, it is instructive to consider briefly the course his meditation could take. If he were to "ponder on the entire past" allowing "the outline of the whole" to emerge ("Flight of the Duchess," ll. 677, 681), he might arrive at a new insight about himself. Browning often allows his characters final moments of truth. He assumes that it is always possible for a man to transcend his temporal identity and, oblivious of the melodrama, he treats a man's last moments as only the most urgent opportunity for self-assessment. Paracelsus, for example, discovers a worth in his years of struggle which he had not previously recognized; and the beaten Gautier admits his lie to Count Gismond, thereby avoiding "God's second death!" (l. 100). Whether final re-visions are positive or negative, the truth itself is saving; and the Bishop of St. Praxed's might, in a moment of intense humiliation, recognize the futility of his competitiveness. The man who preaches with real eloquence about "Vanity" might conclude in tones like these: "Gazing up into the darkness I saw myself as a creature driven and derided by vanity; and my eyes burned with anguish and anger."[4] Such an awareness would be tantamount to a deathbed conversion.

But none of this happens. Instead, the Bishop pursues a course analogous to that adopted in "A Toccata of Galuppi's." Stimulated by Galuppi's music, the speaker muses on Venetian frivolity—"Dust and ashes, dead and done with, Venice spent what Venice earned"(l. 35)— and the general fact of mutability. Soon the toccata seems to urge the listener's own mortality and to challenge his smug intellectualism:

> you know physics, something of geology,
> Mathematics are your pastime; souls shall rise in their degree;
> Butterflies may dread extinction,—you'll not die, it cannot be!
> (ll. 37–39).

The sarcasm is so clear, the implication ought to be unevadable. But the listener deflects the taunt by the simple expedient of reverting to the Venetians. He conjures up the "Dear dead women" (l. 44), sentimentalizes over their magnificent hair and abundant bosoms, and refuses to criticize them. This gentlemanly mellowness is strategically self-serving; for in sparing the women, he closes the subject altogether and spares himself. He may feel "chilly" at the end of the poem, but he suffers no serious metaphysical shudder. The dying Bishop, of course, has more to resist than a musically induced *frisson*. He labors with greater urgency to ignore disturbing truths, and his monologue represents one of Browning's major successes in the genre of the confession manqué.

The most glaring fact about the Bishop of St. Praxed's is that he is a covetous man, one whose appetite is whetted by others' desire. Even his mistress is regarded with the satisfaction of a successful collector; "She, men would have to be your mother once, / Old Gandolf envied me, so fair she was!" (ll. 4–5). His acquisitiveness makes him interpret Gandolf's death as a maneuver to secure a desirable bit of ecclesiastical real estate:

> —Old Gandolf cozened me, despite my care;
> Shrewd was that snatch from out the corner South
> He graced his carrion with, God curse the same!   (ll. 17–19).

To avenge himself for the loss of the niche, the Bishop plans to sneer everlastingly upon Gandolf's "paltry onion-stone" (l. 31). Even the lump of lapis lazuli shall serve as a post-mortem taunt: "So, let the blue lump poise between my knees, / . . . / For Gandolf shall not choose but see and burst!" (ll. 47, 50).

Another element of the Bishop's make-up is his exuberant sensuousness. His description of the initial version of his tomb is remarkable for its kinetic energy; "Peach-blossom marble all, the rare, the ripe / As fresh-poured red wine of a mighty pulse" (ll. 29–30). His colors, as Park Honan notes, "are themselves objets d'art . . . , he treats them lovingly, almost ecstatically, moving through a kind of luscious chromatic gallery of them."[5] He treats them, one might add, as does Browning himself, who once confessed

> to a Chinese love for bright red—the very names "vermilion" "scarlet" warm me,—yet in this cold climate nobody wears red to comfort one's eye save soldiers and fox hunters, and old women fresh from a Parish Christmas Distribution of cloaks. To dress in floating loose crimson silk, I almost understand being a Cardinal![6]

The Bishop's reaction to the incense of a pontifical high Mass is similarly intense, suggesting a robust love of strong sensations. But the fact is that the Bishop's appreciation is inherently limited. In Browning's view a man may have keen observational powers and still fail to know reality; his reactions to the physical universe may be powerful and yet ultimately inadequate. Some of Browning's most ignorant characters are, in their own ways, pleasurably alive to their surroundings. An "Italian Person of Quality," for example, is thrilled by the turmoil of the city square where, among other goings-on, "the travelling doctor gives pills, lets blood, draws teeth" ("Up at a Villa,"

l. 41). And Caliban, entranced by the swirls of the ocean current and the webbing effect of sunlight, admires the "meshes of fire, some great fish breathes at times" (l. 14). Even Sludge insists on the minuteness of his attention to external reality:

> One man lives fifty years in ignorance
> Whether grass be green or red,—"No kind of eye
> For colour," say you; while another picks
> And puts away even pebbles, when a child,
> Because of bluish spots and pinky veins.   (ll. 868–72).

But Browning distinguishes the varieties of sensuousness. "Up at a Villa" faults the chaotic excitability of its speaker; he is, after all, scornfully indifferent to the wild rural tulip that "blows out its great red bell / Like a thin clear bubble of blood" (ll. 24–25). As the stunning image suggests, the gentleman is neglecting glory. His zesty urban impressionability reduces to a childish love of distraction and is easily distinguished from the true power of "scenting the world, looking it full in face" ("How it Strikes a Contemporary," l. 11).

The limitations of Caliban's sensibility become clear upon comparison with Saul's David. The latter surrenders to the objects of his attention; his kind of sympathy respects the independence of reality. Caliban, however, treats the universe as an extension of himself and attributes to creatures a recognizably borrowed life. The fish he spots in the icy water is thought of as longing

> to 'scape the rock stream . . .
> And thaw herself within the lukewarm brine
> O' the lazy sea.   (ll. 34–36).

Her longing is meaningful to Caliban only as an emblem of his own restlessness. He even ascribes his ambivalence to her. Debarred from a life which allures him, that of Prospero and Miranda, Caliban assumes that the fish is repelled by warm water and sees her flouncing back from "bliss she was not born to breathe/ . . . / Hating and loving warmth alike" (ll. 41, 43). Participation of this sort involves transferred impressions; and because Caliban does not recognize his superimposition for what it is, he fails to understand either himself or the life around him. Imagination is not, for him, a way to truth.

Sludge's way of "noticing"—he uses this verb repeatedly—is

similarly inadequate. His interest in the universe is distorted by his monstrous egotism:

> My care is for myself;
> Myself am whole and sole reality
> Inside a raree-show and market-mob
> Gathered about it.   (ll. 908–11).

Unable to suspend his self-concern, he projects his non-essential little anxieties onto the world. For him, to notice means to allegorize, to reduce a universe of fine details to foolish and petty significance. He believes that reality is fraught with meaning; but unlike David or Fra Lippo Lippi, Sludge has no idea that it might be a moral meaning. He assumes that phenomena are personal signs and finds messages about haircuts. Though few characters seem more conspicuously unlike than the medium and St. Praxed's Bishop, the quality of their response to the world is similar. Neither has a sense of the integrity of phenomena, of the interiority of things outside himself. Browning indicates the limits of the bishop's sensuousness by making him overly and almost irrelevantly attentive to surfaces. In a line that is weighted with consecutive stresses, he imagines women with "great smooth marbly limbs" (l. 75) thereby reducing human beings to emphatically sculptural beauties. His love of objects is equally faulty; his appreciation of the lapis involves a ghastly juxtaposition. He remembers it as "Big as a Jew's head cut off at the nape, / Blue as a vein o'er the Madonna's breast" (ll. 43–44). Even the bishop's connoisseurship is the result of his imaginative impoverishment. Sensuous stimulation awakens in him an overwhelming desire to own the stimulant, not the desire to possess it in any profound sense. He, like the medium, feels the need to appropriate what he cannot genuinely know. What Sludge attempts by interpretation, the bishop essays by theft or purchase. But neither strategy is illuminating, and the Bishop's acquisitive relationship with reality is no more valid than Sludge's mediumship.

As the bishop talks on, his mind wanders. A fine stroke of psychological naturalism, this confusion enables Browning to dramatize, within the poem itself, the inadequacy of the bishop's sensibility. His imagination ranges irrepressibly, but its very insatiability implies its faultiness. Instinctively, the bishop protects himself from the oblivion of death, from the effacement of his own identity, by

falling back on old habits; he mandates a permanent and immortal-
izing possession. His need to have is exaggerated because he is about to
pass, stripped and possessionless, into the void. The opulence of his
marble, jasper and lapis tombs serves the double purpose of demon-
strating his power and his dread. No single conceivable tomb arrests
his vagrant imagination, because none is sufficient to keep him alive.
As he composes successive variations, bringing each into focus and
then allowing it to fade, he manages to evade the discovery that his
preoccupation is "Vanity."

In his final muddling of consciousness, the bishop falls prey to the
tendency of the unknown painter; he identifies with an artifact. In life
he has made the mistake of defining himself in terms of ownership;
now, in death, he can no longer distinguish between possessor and
possession. Obsessed with the idea of a tomb, he imaginatively petrifies
and finally mistakes himself for his own effigy.[7] He begins this process
aware that he is manipulating a figure of speech:

> For as I lie here, hours of the dead night,
> Dying in state and by such slow degrees,
> I fold my arms as if they clasped a crook,
> And stretch my feet forth straight as stone can point,
> And let the bedclothes, for a mortcloth, drop
> Into great laps and folds of sculptor's-work: (ll. 85–90).

But soon he speaks as if he were in fact lying on the entablature await-
ing his death. He asks his sons to

> heighten my impoverished frieze
> . . . .
> To comfort me on my entablature
> Whereon I am to lie till I must ask
> "Do I live, am I dead?"   (ll. 104, 111–13).

What begins as a similitude ends in confusion and he believes himself
in the niche opposite Gandolf:

> and, going, turn your backs
> —Ay, like departing altar-ministrants,
> And leave me in my church, the church for peace.
>   (ll. 120–22).

The bishop eventually becomes aware that he will not have a fine tomb, but only "gritstone, a-crumble!" (l. 116). Driven by this deprivation to a final act of evasion, he attempts once more to define himself in terms of something outside the self. In the last lines of the poem, blind to the ironies of his desperate maneuver, the bishop turns his attention to his mistress. His earlier candor about the woman's possible infidelity— "sons mine . . . ah God, I know not!" (l. 3)—is irrelevant to his dire need. He supposes that he cannot lose what is already lost—"she is dead beside, / Dead long ago" (ll. 5–6)—and he comforts himself in his usual way. He rejoices, not that she was fair, but that Gandolf "envied me, so fair she was!" (l.125). His obsession with having and competing operates finally to prevent his epiphany. He, like the unknown painter, concludes his monologue embracing a delusion and fending off truth. But this successful resistance is a Pyrrhic victory. Saved from shame only to be morally lost, the Bishop is ultimately self-defeated.

Defensiveness in Browning's poetry is nearly always counterproductive. He regards it as inevitably falsifying. Nowhere is this more evident than in "Bishop Blougram's Apology." Rhetorically wily and engaging, Blougram justifies himself using his critic's "own premise" (l. 171). Less interested in truth than in victory, Blougram wants to extract Gigadibs' approval on the journalist's own terms. He does not attempt, therefore, to explain his personal faith; instead he defends his prelatic commitment as intellectually coherent and socially deployable. He makes his case without ever establishing his religious integrity. It is evident, despite the title of the poem, that Blougram's speech is an apology only insofar as it attempts, as Arnold Shapiro writes, "to convert Gigadibs—to a new respect for his host."[8] Blougram is not examining himself for the sake of his own soul or even defending himself to his own satisfaction. His speech is an avowed misrepresentation and is not likely to alter his self-assessment.

Blougram even indicates, with complacent and soothing anaphora, the slight chance of any spiritual change:

> Thus I am made, thus life is best for me,
> And thus that it should be I have procured;
> And thus it could not be another way,
> I venture to imagine.   (ll. 337–40).

And while his culminating assertion is no surprise—"My business is not to remake myself" (l. 354)—it is cause for alarm.[9] Such stolidity, if weighed against Browning's concern with conversion, is ominous. His characters typically need re-creating and ought not to be too serenely pleased with themselves. For a man to insist that his condition is inevitable, fixed, or "best" may be a way of evading quite the opposite truth. The most extreme example of such a tactic is Johannes Agricola's antinomianism. Obsessed with the idea of corruption and sin, but unable to confront his own evil, he fanatically denies the possibility of perversion:

> I have God's warrant, could I blend
> >All hideous sins, as in a cup,
> >To drink the mingled venoms up;
> Secure my nature will convert
> >The draught to blossoming gladness fast.   (ll. 33–37).

He attempts to forestall reasonable objections by attributing his purity to God's inscrutable will. Less exaggerated, but just as strategic, is Andrea del Sarto's assertion that his life is divinely determined:

> >Love, we are in God's hand.
> How strange now, looks the life he makes us lead;
> So free we seem, so fettered fast we are!
> I feel he laid the fetter: let it lie!   (ll. 49–52).

By attributing his personal limitations to a divine fetter, Andrea is free to express satisfaction with what ought to dissatisfy him; and like Blougram he can deny the need for any change:

> >I am grown peaceful as old age tonight.
> I regret little, I would change still less.
> Since there my past life lies, why alter it?   (ll. 244–46).

In the course of their monologues, both the painter and the Bishop appear to review the important choices made in their lives. But neither is really in touch with his past. Each is busy resisting the "ugly consequence" ("Blougram," l. 160) of his own hypocrisy or mediocrity.

It should be noted, too, that the apparent passivity of Andrea and Blougram is far different from that of Browning's potential converts.

The latter, like Saul or the Duchess, are psychically defenseless and ready for renewal. Their morale is so low that self-esteem presents no obstacle to change. The Bishop and the painter, however, cling to their identities. Blougram may be at ease, but he is never off guard. Having vigorously "procured" his station in life, he maintains himself by accepting the *status quo*. Andrea's peacefulness is equally defensive. He submits to what he regards as an imposed condition to protect the illusion of his artistic genius.

In some of Browning's poems, defensiveness takes the form of deferral, and the self-esteem which impedes conversion is sometimes based on legitimate attainments. In "An Epistle . . . of Karshish," for example, the Arab's resistance to the tale of Lazarus stems, in part, from his skill as a physician. Prepared to accept new cures, he prefers not to entertain the possibility of a miracle and forestalls consideration of Lazarus' belief.

Karshish begins routinely and, with strict control, postpones explaining "what set [him] off a-writing first of all" (l. 66). Lazarus has just left him, and Karshish is in the first flush of bewilderment over this strangely arresting man. His 61-line delay is purposeful, for he hopes to absorb the impact of Lazarus' innocence and consider the case without acknowledging his unsettled response. His diction, as Park Honan notes, especially the colloquial "a-writing" with its "air of casualness," is a sign of Karshish's "reluctance to admit . . . the profoundly serious nature of his report."[10] Even his echoes of the Epistles (II. Corinthians 11:23–33 and Romans 1: 1–7) indicate, as Richard D. Altick remarks, "that in certain crucial respects Karshish was *not* like St. Paul."[11] When Karshish finally does bring himself to speak of Lazarus, he breaks off with a pair of tensely impatient short questions: "why all this of what he saith? / Why write of trivial matters?" (ll. 277–78). The reader wonders, why indeed; what is the motive of this epistle? Karshish's account is apologetic and guarded, but not because it is a public utterance; he has no confidence that his epistle will reach Abib. His caution is a mode of repression. Hoping to manage and conceal from himself the excitement this man arouses, he speaks of Lazarus with disdain: "after all, our patient . . . / Is stark mad; should we count on what he says?" (ll. 263–4). But he is of two minds about the man and the very reluctance of his epistle suggests fascination and unconscious worry.

As a medical man "not incurious in God's handiwork" (1.2)

Karshish expects a natural explanation of Lazarus' resurrection. Predisposed to regard Christ as a physician, he writes of Him as a superior sage who through some "stroke of art / Unknown" (ll. 83–84) can dramatically heal mania; such art " 't were well to know" (1. 84). The irrational excitement Karshish refuses to confront proves strong enough to disturb his professional calm and to interrupt his flow of words. Here, as so often in Browning's poems, the intrusive is associated with the truthful; the unconscious, with the uncompromised. The physician's inadvertent hearkening back to the man Lazarus is more authentic than his calm examination of the evidence of the cure. Karshish supposes that truth has to do with his competencies, with his comprehensive system of medical thought, with his empirical and heretofore fully serviceable method of negotiating with reality. He can, as a doctor, interpret the facts of this case. But his patterned and comfortable modes of thought cannot accommodate Lazarus' personal convictions. Hence Karshish's anxiety; the encounter with Lazarus sets him on dubious new terms with himself.

Browning is interested in legitimate impediments to truth, not simply in fears and illusions. In "An Epistle . . . of Karshish" he examines the paradox that a man's vested interest in his own expertise may be a source of self-division; his genuine capabilities may be self-alienating. Karshish's medical skill puts him frighteningly at odds with his longing for knowledge "increased beyond the fleshly faculty" (1. 140). His professional role generally serves him well, but there is an unacknowledged inner self who responds to Lazarus and threatens the physician's public identity. To acknowledge his desire for contact with transcendence, to admit that an unreasonable mystery is attractive, is also to admit something that discredits him. Browning regards the Arab's dilemma as representative. His self-division is not attributable to some peculiar unfitness; it is inherently normal for a man to resist the truth he longs to embrace.

Karshish knows that Lazarus believes the Nazarene to be "God himself" (1. 268). His observation that Lazarus does not affect

> to preach
> The doctrine of his sect whate'er it be,
> Make proselytes as madmen thirst to do   (ll. 213–15)

adds an important element to Browning's theory of conversion. In

Christmas-Eve the narrator discusses the inefficacy of the evangelical preacher's technique and concludes firmly that citations and proofs are "abundantly convincing" only to "those convinced before" (1. 269). Even Christ, the best of teachers, could not move men with the "mere exposition of morality" (1. 1030). It is his life that furnishes the "motive" and "injunction" (1. 1043) for his followers:

> Believe in me,
> Who lived and died, yet essentially
> Am Lord of Life. . . .   (ll. 1054–56).

This challenge accomplishes the "real God-function" (1. 1040) of converting the whole man. It is a similar kind of appeal that affects Karshish. Lazarus' refusal to proselytize gives the Arab pause; he wonders about the means of transferring one's private assent: "How can he give his neighbour the real ground, / His own conviction?" (ll. 216–17). And, without knowing it, Karshish answers his own question. Not only does he feel the attractiveness of the Nazarene's teaching—"The very God! think Abib; dost thou think? / So, the All-Great, were the All-Loving too" (ll. 304–5)—he is profoundly disturbed by Lazarus' manner. The man's entire bearing serves as witness to the depth of his belief; he has "something in the look of him" (1. 69). The world may regard Lazarus as a fool, but he takes no cognizance: "Call his great truth a lie, why, still the old / 'Be it as God please' " (ll. 218–219). He cannot prove that Christ is divine any more than Caponsacchi can prove Pompilia's innocence; in each case the proof adduced is the force with which the individual communicates his personal conviction. The energy Lazarus possesses is that of radical passivity. Completely uninterested in defending himself, he has an effaced but unshakable self-regard. His obliviousness to the world's skepticism is eloquent, implying what the seer of "Pisgah-Sights. II" openly proclaims: "Just a discerner, / I would teach no one" (ll. 19–20). Lazarus moreover, is "witness of the size, the sum, / The value in proportion of all things" (ll. 143–44). Karshish recognizes that the "discerner" is not disoriented but primally re-oriented. The world to him is transparent, and he behaves as if the earth were "forced on [his] soul's use while seeing heaven" (1. 142). It is this condition, the undeniably total alteration of Lazarus' perception, that unsettles the physician.

Just as Karshish postpones introducing his subject, so too he delays his conclusion. He tries to cut his epistle short, promising to write again from Jerusalem, then adds a second, enigmatic "It is strange." Such closure leaves some readers dissatisfied; Roma King, for example, speaks of Browning's willingness "to sacrifice ideological and moral completeness to psychological intensity."[12] But this criticism is too end-directed; it ignores the fact that incompleteness and inhibition are the poem's chief concern. By the last line of his epistle, Karshish has a new sense of his inner need and the limitations of his intellectual system. An obstacle to conversion still looms, however, in the form of anxiety about his identity. An irrational being with transcendent longings, he prefers to think of himself as an itinerant empiricist; and now that the discrepancy is exposed, the physician has two alternatives. He can acknowledge his need to believe or make a habit of delay. After Jerusalem he will be a convert or a chronic, but uncommitted, skeptic.

In "The Statue and the Bust," Browning considers the consequences of repeated delay. His theme is the opportunity that is never seized and the terrible results of permanent deferral. The story of Duke Ferdinand and the Riccardi bride begins with a moment of recognition:

> He looked at her, as a lover can;
> She looked at him, as one who awakes:
> The past was a sleep, and her life began.   (ll. 28–30).

Their shared glance seems to have the force of a call to new life, and the lady believes that in discovering the Duke she has also discovered her true identity. Such an awareness, if authentic, amounts to an obligation; "The end of life being manifest" (l. 224), the lady and her Duke must act. But should they discover they have mistaken one another, they must relinquish their identification as lovers. There can be no doubt about Browning's feelings on this matter, for Elizabeth draws him out on the subject of "jilts" in the course of their own courtship. She writes:

> Then I will confess to you that all my life long I have had a rather strange sympathy & dyspathy—the sympathy having concerned the genus *jilt* (as vulgarly called) male and female—and the dyspathy the

whole class of heroically virtuous persons who make sacrifices of what they call 'love' to what they call 'duty.' . . . I have always & shall always understand how it is possible for the most earnest & faithful of men & even of women perhaps, to err in the convictions of the heart as well as of the mind, to profess an affection which is an illusion, and to recant & retreat loyally at the eleventh hour, on becoming aware of the truth which is in them. Such men are the truest of men, . . & the most courageous for the truth's sake, . . & instead of blaming them I hold them in honour. . . .[13]

and Browning concurs:

. . . do you suppose we differ on so plain a point as that of the superior wisdom, and generosity, too, of announcing such a change &c at the eleventh hour? There can be no doubt of it. . . .[14]

On one occasion he even explains how he hopes he would behave should he discover he no longer loved her:

. . . I will fancy I lose my head and love you no longer . . . and then (which is *now*) . . . now, do you think I am so poor a creature as to go on adding to my faults, and letting you gently down, as the phrase is, with cowardly excuses, "postponing" this, and "consenting to delay" the other,—and perhaps managing to get you to do the whole business for me in the end? I hope & think I should say at once—Oh, no more of this![15]

But the lovers in the poem neither elope nor recant; instead they use the "postponing" strategy that tacitly permits the Riccardi husband to incarcerate his wife:

Calmly he said that her lot was cast,
That the door she had passed was shut on her
Till the final catafalk repassed.   (ll. 55–57).

Her chamber is thus a premature grave and she regards her window as a "loop of hell / Whence a damned soul looks on paradise!" (ll. 68–69). Flight, under these circumstances, is equated with life, and the poem is less concerned with the morality of adultery than with the problem of fidelity to the self. If the lady's love is genuine, her delay is not, as is sometimes suggested, a matter of furtively "cherishing an unlawful love," but rather an acceptance of living death.[16] Her daily unwillingness to alter her circumstances is a form of self-betrayal. If, however, her love is merely an illusion, then she is guilty of vitiating her own life. Browning reinforces this interpretation with a reference to a parable of the Second Coming. The lovers' sin is "the unlit lamp and the ungirt loin" (l. 247). They, like the virgins and servants in the gospel, are in a condition of ultimate unreadiness. They come to the moment of crisis unwilling to embrace or reject one another.

The hesitation of the lady and her Duke dramatizes the difference between knowledge and incentive, between ambiguous and ardent desire. The description of the lady's daily watch at her window sheds some light on the nature of her weakness. The square the Duke crosses is compared to a book that contains

> one picture and only one,
> Which daily to find she undertook:
>
> When the picture was reached the book was done,
> And she turned from the picture at night to scheme
> Of tearing it out for herself next sun.   (ll. 146–50).

This reduction of her "book" to one page of illustration has two implications. It suggests that escape is within her power, for the tearing of a picture from a text is not an impossible task; and it hints at the reason for her failure to act. In her growing paralysis she turns to the Duke's "picture" in much the same way that the unknown painter returns to his "same series, Virgin, Babe and Saint" (l. 60). Both use monotony and repetition to avoid taking risks. But here the similarity ends, for the lady is a voyeur, not an artist. Soothing herself with a daily glimpse of her lover, she tries to make her opportunity permanent without ever making it obligatory. Valuing the Duke's predictability in lieu of intimacy, she settles for pattern instead of life.

Even her nocturnal scheming serves, almost perversely, to delay her flight and to maintain her role—at some level it is a desired role— as a Riccardi wife. Her constant but ineffectual planning prevents her from reaching the consciously helpless condition that results in unambiguous desire. Were the lady to feel totally powerless, like the narrators of *Pauline* or "By the Fire-side," she would have fantasies of rescue and conferred gratification. The very extremity of her condition would be purifying. If she could not even conceive how to satisfy her needs, her desire could not be dissipated. But this is not the case; the lady is politic and her secret designs are a subtle form of default. Instead of love and salvation, she and her Duke accept separation—both here and hereafter. The crypt-like isolation of the lady's room is exchanged for that of separate graves, and the narrator fancies how the lovers wait the "trump of doom" (1. 214). Because they have foregone their apocalyptic chance in life, he is sure they are excluded after death from the company of the "soldier-saints" (1. 222).

Despite the contradiction of their enacted identities, the Duke and the lady suppose they are true lovers. Time, however, exaggerates the distance between illusion and reality and precipitates a partial discovery. The lady is forced by her mirror to relinquish the image of herself as a lover; and, since she has never consciously accepted herself as a wife, she feels suddenly bereft of identity:

> One day . . . the lady saw her youth
> Depart. . . .
> . . . .
> And wondered who the woman was,
> Hollow-eyed and haggard-cheeked,
>
> Fronting her silent in the glass.   (ll. 157–8, 161–63).

But she finds "a thing to do" ("Porphyria's Lover," 1. 38); and both she and the Duke seem to achieve a degree of self-awareness. She commissions and compares herself to a lifeless "lady of clay" (1. 186) and he orders a bronze. Yet there is something ambiguous about these gestures of self-condemnation. The irony of immortalizing their wasted youth and beauty is not completely honest; it smacks of morbid sentimentality. They preserve, in bronze and marble stateliness, the likenesses that remind them of what they choose to think they might have been. The tenuousness of this procedure is pathetic, but sufficient to prevent more devastating admissions. Their self-accusations reinforce their illusions, and the statue and the bust prevent them from recognizing the spuriousness of their identification as lovers. In Browning's view, criticism is sometimes the most refined form of delusion. Pseudo-lovers, like pseudo-artists, defend themselves from dreaded truths by conceding lesser faults. The bride and the Duke, like the "Pictor Ignotus," resort to self-repudiation as a tactic. The painter admits that his work is monotonous; the lovers admit delay. Such confessions are painful, but skewed and protective; and the "thought which saddens while it soothes" ("Pictor Ignotus," l. 3) is not an epiphany, but an evasion.

The master in Browning's canon of the strategic self-indictment is the vulnerable Andrea del Sarto. As uneasily complacent as the "Pictor Ignotus," Andrea borrows his technique of mild accusation. Confronted with the failure of dull achievement, he bolsters his threatened self-esteem with an ironically successful confession manqué. At the opening of his poem, Andrea placates the angry Lucrezia by agreeing to one of her arranged commissions. But this blatant prostitution of his art rankles. In need of soothing, he proceeds with apparent thoroughness to console himself with confession and self-appraisal. In surveying his merits and defects, however, he manages to avoid the truth about himself, and his meditation proves evasively deceptive.

When he boasts to the uninterested Lucrezia of his legitimate skill in draftsmanship, he makes the damaging admission that he is frequently disengaged from his work:

> I can do with my pencil what I know,
> What I see, what at bottom of my heart
> I wish for, if I ever wish so deep—   (ll. 60–62).

This remark, which seems a proof of Andrea's veracity, is a sample of the subtle dishonesty whereby he sustains the illusion of his visionary power. Smoothed with a tell-tale symmetry and rehearsed glide, it is a ploy to forestall criticism. If a sketch seems uninspired, he has already admitted, like the unknown painter, that his heart is sometimes not in his work. It also solicits praise by seizing on the nearly universal discrepancy between what a man can be and what he is. Although Browning's renewals all depend on the discontinuity of the genuine and the apparent identity, Andrea's comment is distressing because the painter is content with the inconsistency. It enables him to identify, not with the "low-pulsed" (l. 82) technician his work publicly proclaims him to be, but with the unrecognized seer who could, even though he does not, look into his heart to paint. Andrea even supposes, fondly remembering Michelangelo's faint praise, that the great man believes him a true artist:

> For, do you know, Lucrezia, as God lives,
> Said one day Agnolo his very self,
> To Rafael . . . I have known it all these years
> . . . .
> "Friend, there's a certain sorry little scrub
> Goes up and down our Florence, none cares how,
> Who, were he set to plan and execute
> As you are, pricked on by your popes and kings,
> Would bring the sweat into that brow of yours!"   (ll. 183–93).

Andrea knows, however, how poorly he conducted himself when King Francis "set [him] to plan and execute" at Fontainebleau. It is typical and also strategic that Andrea's version of Michelangelo's remark emphasizes the disparity between scrub and artist. The compliment which might have served as a stimulus or prompted a request for criticism—"Do, for the poor obstructed artist's sake, / Go with him over that spoiled work" (*The Ring and the Book*, X. 1571–2) —works instead to destroy incentive; while offering recognition, it makes opportunity safely implausible. The force of the praise is further blunted by time; it is new to Lucrezia, but Andrea has "known it," hoarded and deadened it "all these years" (l. 185).

The fumbling efforts of Andrea's rivals, the young painters who agonize over preliminary sketches but fail to draw their figures properly, elicit another surprising but unconsciously strategic assertion. Despite their faults of execution, these others, he concedes, are prompted by a passion that he lacks; "There burns a truer light of God" in them than in himself (l. 79). Such self-deprecation, "all the play, the insight and the stretch / Out of me, out of me" (ll. 116–17), brings him to the brink of genuine assessment. But just as Andrea seems about to discover the reasons for his mediocrity, to examine his soul and find it wanting, he swerves. Ignoring the spectre of primal artistic inadequacy, he refuses to confront the terrible possibility that he, regardless of the circumstances inhibiting or abetting his art, lacks imaginative power. Instead, he pursues the more flattering assumption buried within his remark: "And wherefore out?" (l. 117). What he lost he must originally have possessed. Because Andrea prefers to think he fell, and not that he was born impaired, it is necessary to account for his loss of "stretch." His entire monologue is an attempt to construct a myth that would spare him a recognition too painful to live with. Because he cannot sustain epiphany, he seizes almost gratefully on the chance to chronicle the decline of his putative genius.

The subsequent review of his life, conducted with patently self-justifying intentions, does not provoke any illumination. From the outset, Andrea's complex defensiveness allows him to adjust all facts. It is clear, for example, that at Francis' court, where all possible encouragement was provided, Andrea's early aspiration to greatness faded. It is important to notice the strange tentativeness with which he records the level of inspiration achieved during his "kingly days" (1. 165); "I surely then could sometimes leave the ground" (1. 151). His very prominence and the monarch's patronage proved threatening. The timid Andrea, instead of embracing his fear, boldly risking failure, and rapturously painting his way to self-knowledge, succumbed to a general failure of nerve. He dreaded finding that he could not, under any circumstances, achieve what his self-esteem required. So he fore-closed all opportunity. To maintain a permanent sense of the visionary option, he removed himself from the supporting context of France to the merely surrounding and even hostile city of Florence; "I am some-thing underrated here, / Poor this long while, despised, to speak the truth" (ll. 143–44). Stealing Francis' gold was Andrea's way of burning bridges; the theft placed an insurmountable obstacle between him and the challenge of achievement. Andrea relishes the guilt that comes with crime; ominous walls of gold protect him from the "humane great monarch's golden look" (1. 153):

> oft at nights
> When I look up from painting, eyes tired out,
> The walls become illumined, brick from brick
> Distinct, instead of mortar, fierce bright gold,
> That gold of his I did cement them with! (ll. 214–18).

Andrea's current need, this evening's quarrel, causes him to linger elegiacally over what, he convinces himself, might have been. He seeks to recover the "festal year" (1. 150) and, if only for a moment, the precious illusion of his ecstatic relationship with Francis:

> One arm about my shoulder, round my neck,
> The jingle of his gold chain in my ear,
> I painting proudly with his breath on me.   (ll. 156–58).

Then with self-serving clarity he recalls the restlessness of his beloved and vitiates the memory of his flight. Though her call permitted his timely escape from France, Andrea prefers to think that he abandoned imminent triumph. Luxuriating in the notion of willfully abrogated opportunity, he pretends that he sacrificed art for love:

> You called me, and I came home to your heart.
> The triumph was—to reach and stay there; since
> I reached it ere the triumph, what is lost?   (ll. 172–74).

Lucrezia, according to Andrea's view, is his artistic nemesis, and his confession to her is an act of aggression. Whining that her inadequacy is the cause of his, he implies that her "perfect brow" conceals an empty head. She cannot replace the incentives that the court once supplied:

> Had you . . . but brought a mind!
> Some women do so. Had the mouth there urged
> "God and the glory! never care for gain."
> . . . .
> I might have done it for you.   (ll. 126–32).

Such a complaint, however, is fallacious; for as David Shaw points out

> Lucrezia can deny for herself the antecedent, and when she negates the consequent, the cause of Andrea's failure seems to follow. But the hypothetical syllogism takes the form of *if* p, *then* q; *but not* p, *therefore not* q, which is invalid. The formal fallacy overlooks the possibility that there may be other causes of Andrea's failure.[17]

It need only be added that Andrea's argument errs by assertion as well as omission, for it misrepresents the role of the woman as muse. The beloved is not capable of bestowing vision—though that is how she is sometimes represented. Her true function is that of recipient; in loving her, the artist achieves a level of self-intimacy that is a necessary condition of vision. She puts him in touch with his innermost self, with the force that organizes his perception of reality. A woman may serve, therefore, as a muse long before she encourages, acknowledges, or even knows the lover. Her love is almost irrelevant, for it is in reaching out to her that the artist becomes self-aware and unperplexed. Browning, it should be remembered, once wrote to Elizabeth, "I loved you from my soul, and gave you my life, so much of it as you would take,—and all that is done, not to be altered now; it was, in the nature of the proceeding, wholly independent of any return on your part."[18] Andrea, however, alleges that Lucrezia has failed him; and to assuage the fear of his own incompetence, he accuses her of the one kind of betrayal she cannot really commit.

This unsubtle indictment of his wife raises the question of motive. Andrea risks angering the woman he has just placated, and can hardly expect this account of his abandoned chance for greatness to elicit her gratitude. He has, however, a powerful, though more oblique, reason for rehearsing his complaints; her acknowledgment of his sacrifice enhances the illusion that his loss was real. Lucrezia serves his evasive purposes by accepting or by simply not challenging his version of the past. Even her inattentiveness, provided it is not mercilessly blatant, can be construed as a serviceable response. Her lack of interest, in fact, is necessary; Andrea confesses to her but is in fear of being truly found out. He wants, therefore, not her intimate sympathy, but merely the appearance of it. Her silence is interpreted as ratification.

Andrea's meditation involves more than just transferred accusations; he invokes the myth of the world well lost for love. Unwilling to admit he needs the relief that submersion in this marriage brings, he chooses to believe that Lucrezia is worth the sacrifice of his art. He pretends to be satisfied with, and in a pathetic way he actually does welcome, this distracting involvement. The pressures of this marital *cul-de-sac* rescue him from anxiety inducing prominence and he welcomes the deprivation. He exults over his wife's beauty and his supposedly absolute possession of her; "Let my hands frame your face in your hair's gold, / You beautiful Lucrezia that are mine!" (ll. 175–76). He enslaves himself to the illusion of her fidelity and makes love to a composite fiction. She is the model for his virgins but also the "snare" (l. 125) and "serpentining beauty" (l. 26) of his private enactment of the fall. He suggests her voluptuous dependence on him—"Your soft hand is a woman of itself, / And mine the man's bared breast she curls inside" (ll. 21–22)—and carefully disguises his plea for her cooperation. He reminds her gently of the external signs of matrimonial harmony and stage-manages their reconciliation scene. Explaining precisely how he wants her to sit with her hand in his, "Both of one mind, as married people use" (l. 16), he secures her compliance with the promise that this charade will refresh him; "I might get up to-morrow to my work / Cheerful and fresh as ever" (ll. 18–19). Andrea's earnings provide her with new frills and pay her lover's debts; all this is implicit in his tactful urging, "To-morrow, how you shall be glad for this!" (l. 20). She is coaxed to tolerate his visual caresses with the reminder that, since she is his model, his contemplation of her beauty is both necessary and remunerative. He repeatedly instructs her in their lovers' economics:

> Another smile?
> If you would sit thus by me every night
> I should work better, do you comprehend?
> I mean that I should earn more, give you more.   (ll. 204–07).

But Lucrezia is a sharper financier than Andrea. She knows "how the love-account really stands";[19] their marriage is a seller's market and her husband will gladly buy even a poor imitation of domestic bliss. She sits, as he wishes, but with her eyes on the window watching for her lover, wholly unconcerned with Andrea's thoughts about his reputation. In an extreme, when she refuses to spend the rest of the evening with him, he simply ignores the obvious—"Yes / You loved me quite enough" (ll. 257–8)—and pretends to dismiss her, "Go, my Love" (l. 267). The self-deceit and control needed to maintain this charade suggest the terrifying nature of the truth Andrea resists. That this should be a distinctly preferable way of conducting his life bespeaks the proportion of his fear.

Andrea's most dangerous ploy, the one which is potentially apocalyptic, is his refusal to clash openly with Lucrezia. Because a quarrel over her pernicious influence on his art could be annihilating, he avoids provoking her in order to avoid revelation. But on two occasions when he stops blaming her, he comes, by rhetorical accident, perilously close to authentic self-recrimination. When he suspends criticism of her, he is left with dangling accusations. After pressing his charge that she does not inspire him, he fumbles an apology in short evasive phrases, "So it seems; / Perhaps not" (ll. 132–33), and then adds the afterthought, "Beside, incentives come from the soul's self" (l. 134). This brings him almost anticlimactically to the verge of discovery, though even here there is a meliorating confusion. A lack of incentive is not the same thing as a lack of insight. And he quickly takes comfort in the lame generalization that all men are "half-men" (I. 140).

Similarly, when he recalls the decision to leave Fontainebleau and indicts her with a hypothetical "had you not grown restless" (l. 166), he hesitates and admits that her desire echoed his own:

> 'twas right, my instinct said;
> Too live the life grew, golden and not grey,
> And I'm the weak-eyed bat no sun should tempt
> Out of the grange whose four walls make his world.
>
> (ll. 167–70).

He only narrowly avoids dislodging the secret that at his height he feared exposure. Andrea evades the truth he thinks he cannot bear to know. But Browning's implicit argument is that the truth is survivable; honest confession is redemptive. Andrea, however, is too frightened to risk this process. Twice he nearly procures an epiphany by inadvertence, but twice he manages to sustain the myth of his surrender to Lucrezia and thus to preserve his counterfeit sense of potential. Andrea, the moderately accomplished artist and failed husband, wants to believe that he had two mutually exclusive options, greatness or love. His crowning delusion, one he shares with the unknown painter, is that he has willingly chosen his fate. He suggests that in joining Lucrezia he knowingly fulfilled his true destiny, that their marital "twilight-piece" (l. 49) is the summation of "all that [he] was born to be and do" (l. 48). He seems to reconfirm this fatal choice in the final lines of the poem. Imagining a contest in the New Jerusalem, he sees himself defeated by Leonardo, Rafael, and Agnolo:

> the three first without a wife,
> While I have mine! So—still they overcome
> Because there's still Lucrezia,—as I choose.   (ll. 264–66).

But this recognition is only a mock epiphany; it is his way of bolstering the illusion of his now ruined, but once glorious, power. This fantasy invests his act of evasion with a vitality and glamour that are consoling. It gives Andrea a moral and aesthetic stature that he does not have. Although he goes through the motions of reviewing his choice, his evening's meditation is an elaborate prevarication. He does not reveal himself to Lucrezia or to himself but carefully perpetrates a fiction. Introspection, for him, is a link with illusion, and memory a way of keeping the events at Fontainbleau permanently available as a defense against truth.

The self-concern that leads Andrea to misconstrue his past causes some of Browning's characters to misinterpret external reality. In "Caliban upon Setebos," he shows how the needs that distort confession affect an individual's cosmogony as well. Andrea's and Caliban's motives are basically the same, only their methods differ. The limitations the one refuses to acknowledge, the other ascribes to his god. Projection replaces evasion as a delusive strategy, and Setebos is actually Caliban's own self, admired and feared as a deified other.

More powerful and content than Caliban, Setebos is, nonetheless, cold, ill at ease, and far from absolute. He exists in mysterious subordination to the Quiet and his inferiority fascinates Caliban. Assuming that Setebos is dissatisfied with his state but unable to "soar / To what is quiet and hath happy life" (ll. 144–45), Caliban supposes that the god expresses his envy by making a "bauble-world to ape yon real" (l. 147). This world-crafting activity is little more than spiritually impoverished play, a solace for his own insufficiency.

What interests Browning about these speculations is the way Caliban's personality limits his perception. Incapable of any more positive emotion than generalized spite, he cannot conceive of a generous motive for the act of creation. His view of the originating principle, as critics have noted, is outrageously at odds with the traditional notion of generative fecundity.[20] The dialogist of the "Timaeus" and generations of Christian Platonists who follow suppose that "he who did construct [the universe] was good, and in one that is good, no envy of anything ever arises. Being devoid of envy then he desired that everything should be so far as possible like himself."[21] The principle of goodness, in other words, requires that everything should have being. Browning is familiar with this argument and uses it himself on occasion. In "Saul" the non-envious cosmogonic good becomes an all-loving God, and David's own generosity prompts the Platonic intuition that whatever love can conceive must be. The existence of the "good things" already known to man is proof that God must "give one more, the best" (l. 276). Neither Caliban nor his god, however, is moved by any such goodness or fullness. Creation, in Caliban's view, is not the bringing into existence of every possible good; on the contrary, Setebos "made all these and more, / Made all we see, and us, in spite: how else?" (ll. 55–56). The god is thought to be inspired by the inaccessibly worthier reality of the Quiet world and, for the sake of a spurious kind of transcendence, to fashion an imitation world that is deliberately and serviceably diminished. The act of creation is the bestowing of existence on assorted inferiors. Peopled by creatures intentionally made "weaker in most points" (l. 63), Setebos' bauble-world has no teleological purpose. It merely affords endless opportunities for "making and marring" (l. 97).

At the bottom of Caliban's theory is his own inability to establish a truly creative relationship with Prospero's world. He cannot imaginatively locate himself there. Incapable of self-transcendence and genuine expansion of consciousness, he produces only mutilated versions of the reality he cannot penetrate. In a deftly ironic bit of drama Browning allows Caliban to improvise his own counterpart. Compelled by his discontent, he blinds a "lumpish" sea creature, pens it in a hole and calls it by his own name. This charade of self-mastery is wholly inconsequential, however, and leaves Caliban as unenlightened as ever about himself or the beast. But the episode suggests a distinction that is important for Browning's art. A subjective aesthetic leaves one ignorant, whereas true creation, because it requires the suspension of one's habitual identity, is a means of discovery. When the personality of the maker is allowed to dominate, then the created object, whether an artifact or a verbal construct, a world or a world-view, is only a deceitful alternative to reality. This is the paradox of Browning's own practice in the dramatic monologue. True art—and in this sense the most deeply personal—must be impersonal.

Browning brings his point home by dramatizing the results of Caliban's projections upon Setebos and the fallacy of creating in one's own limited image. Not only does Caliban's method leave him ignorant of God, it magnifies the consequences of his inadequate self-apprehension. The degree to which he misunderstands himself is the degree to which the deity frightens him in the closing lines of the poem.

Caliban supposes that his own acts of spite are utterly disinterested, hardly acts of love, but surely not acts of hate. This refusal to confront the demonic in his nature leads to Caliban's victimization. His projected emotions necessarily include those he does not acknowledge, and he is eventually terrified by his own relocated malice. When the tempest arises, he misinterprets it as evidence of Setebos' anger; unwilling to admit that he himself acts punitively, he nevertheless attributes to Setebos his own brand of behavior. Hence the significance of the poem's epigraph, "Thou thoughtest that I was altogether such a one as thyself" (Psalm 50:21).[22] Caliban has, moreover, convincing reasons for expecting vengeance; his frantic, metrically nervous assessment of nature's abrupt change culminates with a pained indication of his motives:

> What, what? A curtain o'er the world at once!
> Crickets stop hissing; not a bird—or, yes,
> There scuds His raven that has told Him all!
> It was fool's play, this prattling!
> . . . .
> . . .Fool to gibe at Him!   (ll. 284–90).

Caliban's attempt to know his god is not an act of love—though this is the usual association in Browning's poetry—but an act of aggression; he assumes from the start that Setebos would be vexed to know of his impudence. Caliban's god is a secretive being who does not reveal himself, except to exact punishment. The irony of Caliban's reaction is that the tempest is not Setebos' doing; the hostility Caliban intuits is a reflection of his own unrecognized vengefulness. His epiphany is a mistake, a projection that leaves him abjectly self-terrorized.

Messages incorrectly attributed to God are not always found in the whirlwind, and in "Mr. Sludge, 'The Medium' " Browning considers the opposite extreme of fraudulent and trivial epiphanies. Intrigued by the many species of falsification, Browning permits his medium to approximate, abuse, and virtually anthologize the confessional strategies of other monologists.

In the beginning of his monologue, Sludge is connivingly self-derogatory. After lying that "this last accident" (l. 6) was his only trick, he proceeds to tell Horsefall "the whole truth, and nought else" (l. 56). Such candor is meant to be disarming and has even elicited, from one critic, the very wrong-headed assertion that of all Browning's characters, Sludge "is the most free from self-delusion and perhaps, psychologically, the healthiest."[23] Sludge's patron turned apprehender wants guilty admissions, and he gets them: "I know 'twas wicked of me" (l. 30); "Cheat's my name" (l. 430). And since confessed wickedness is the traditional prelude to reform, Sludge artfully suggests that Horsefall abandon the role of vengeful "angry gentleman" (l. 27) for that of moral Perseus:

> I mean to change my trade and cheat no more.
> Yes, this time really its upon my soul!
> Be my salvation!—under Heaven of course.   (ll. 62–64).

A scoundrel's escape is thus hastily metamorphosed into an opportunity for rehabilitation. Perhaps Sludge realizes that his vapid assertiveness ("really"), his cliches, and tacked-on pieties are not very convincing, for he strengthens his case by insisting that Horsefall is *obliged* to play savior. He is the original corruptor, the cultivator of the hypothetical David and instructor in "the art of lies" (l. 169). In shaping David's performance, Horsefall and his circle of friends are guilty of perverting the performer:

> David's performance rounds, each chink gets patched
> Every protrusion of a point's filed fine.
> All's fit to set a-rolling round the world,
> And then return to David finally,
> Lies seven-feet thick about his first half inch.   (ll. 238–42).

This crust of lies which comes between Sludge and the audience also separates him from his genuine self. Integrity requires that he distinguish "Sludge as Sludge" (l. 656) from Sludge as showman and that he reject the proposed life of managed performance. But his patrons require that he confuse the circumference with the core:

> When you buy
> The actor's talent, do you dare propose
> For his soul beside? Whereas my soul you buy!
> Sludge acts Macbeth, obliged to be Macbeth,
> Or you'll not hear his first word!   (ll. 648–52).

Because Sludgehood is a constructed, communal phenomenon, because the circle has daintily ignored and also strenuously defended his fraud, Sludge's self-criticism has the force of a group indictment. It is a shrewd ploy. Having every pragmatic reason to tell the worst, he does so with slimy exuberance. The more shocking his contrivance the greater their sin. Because "it's your own fault more than mine" (1. 84), Sludge's corruptor turned captor must be merciful.

In this perverted anti-confession, the most direct self-censure— "I lied, sir—there" (1. 263)—becomes a way of shaming the auditor. Horsefall, like Gigadibs before him, is the victim of a verbal assault. There are similarities with Lucrezia, too, for both the medium and the painter seek their auditor's cooperation. Both use confessional utterance as a way of soliciting future complicity. In the case of Sludge, blackmail is possible because he convinces Horsefall of the latter's genuine faultiness. He has not only malformed David, but by bullying skeptical guests, he has been an active accomplice "in rascality" (l. 373). Confession should, of course, repudiate, not implicate. It should be an occasion for discovering one's deceitfulness and for establishing a kind of self-sovereignty. But Sludge, by insisting on the compelling influence of Horsefall's circle, subverts the confessional enterprise. He gains his escape but misses his epiphany.

In accordance with the technique of the self-aware penitent, Sludge professes to loathe his role. The sentiment, however, is misdirected, for the "showman's ape" (l. 600) discharges a career-long hatred, not of his duplicitous conduct, but of the degradation he must endure. He resents that he is

> Encouraged to be wicked and make sport,
> Fret or sulk, grin or whimper, any mood
> So long as the ape be in it and no man.   (ll. 601–03).

The recognition that he has made his own guilt, that he has cooperated with his deformers, is avoided. He detests them instead of himself. The force of Sludge's manipulative deprecation is compounded by his misogyny:

> Curse your women too,
> Your insolent wives and daughters, that fire up

> Or faint away if a male hand squeeze theirs,
> Yet, to encourage Sludge, may play with Sludge
> As only a "medium", only the kind of thing
> They must humour, fondle . . . oh, to misconceive
> Were too preposterous!   (ll. 608–14).

Sludge's contempt for these hysterical wives and daughters is warranted and yet distracting. His anger over the women's proprietary fondling blocks the acknowledgment that he enjoyed their emasculating attentions.

The extravagance of Sludge's anti-feminine malice raises the general issue of confessional structure. Perhaps the most obvious fact about his monologue is that it is too long; it seems, on first reading, to have only the "casual and fortuitous" shape that J. Hillis Miller attributes to Browning's poetry in general.

> The poem might have been written any number of different ways. It might have been longer or shorter. Its only justification is the fact that this is after all the way it came to Browning, as spontaneously and naturally as the pattern leaves make falling on a pond. There is throughout Browning a kind of anarchy of form and matter. He inherits nothing from the past, trusts every least instinct, and lets his poems grow like lawless sports in nature, unheard-of mutants directed by novel arrangements of chromosomes and efflorescing grotesquely—form, but unlike any other form. At any moment the whole direction of the poem may dynamically shift, and a huge new bubble outburst where was only flat latency before.[24]

Once Sludge has bullied Horsefall sufficiently and knows for certain that he will be allowed to leave Boston, he need only "tell some queer things" (l. 65) and be done. But the monologue is structured by a motive other than the securing of V notes. Confession has left Sludge unsatisfied and he does more than ramble anarchically on; he obsessively begins anew.

In the first half of his poem, he examines but does not abandon his role as medium and is left longing for some kind of legitimacy. Although he foregoes apocalypse, he feels "an anemic but persistent" need to salvage his integrity.[25] Using the confession of his hoaxes as a pledge of his veracity—"believe that: believe this" (l. 804)—he takes a new direction and attempts to negotiate the distance between cheat and seer:

> I don't know, can't be sure
> But there was something in it, tricks and all!
> Really, I want to light up my own mind.   (ll. 808–10).

Having admitted his spuriousness, he boldly suggests that the genuine self may find expression, not through repentant conversion, but in the very act of misrepresentation. It is impossible to tell whether Sludge believes this or not. It may be that this is a refined form of impudence, the final duping of Horsefall, and yet it may be a desperate attempt at self-deceit, or perhaps a sign of Sludge's actual confusion about what is genuine and what is not. His second confession, at any rate, is an attempt to relieve himself of the charge of charlatanism. He argues that he is not a thorough-going fraud, but that his role as trickster is only a socially imposed self-parody. Such a defense is an absolute failure morally. By conceding that he is a pandering illusionist, but brazenly affirming that he is, nonetheless, a true medium, Sludge denies the "abysm" between what he is and what he should be. In so doing, he eliminates the basis of reclamation. By insisting that he is somehow a true medium, he again forestalls the saving acknowledgment of his utter inauthenticity. He merely verbalizes about an integrity he will never acquire and then resumes his degraded role as hoaxer.

"Mr. Sludge, the Medium" is a caveat. For Sludge shows how completely a man's energies for self-discovery can be manipulated. His poem suggests how terribly difficult it is to remedy one's inauthenticity and how easy it is, through false confession, to avoid the admission of disingenuousness. Browning knows that the introspective mode is by no means automatically redeeming. But by acknowledging the perils of the method, by creating his evaders and resisters, he is able to establish the terms on which renewal is to be achieved. The opportunity an unknown painter or a dying bishop squanders is extended to others. The confrontation that the medium or Andrea only approximates, others may fully achieve. Browning's attitude concerning man's potential as a convert is not to be found by tallying up the number of true and false confessions he creates, for he is constantly aware of *both* possibilities. Nor can his assessment of mankind's collective integrity be determined by the ratio of authentic to fraudulent epiphanies he describes. Browning's knowledge of human psychology is too comprehensive to permit simple optimism or pessimism about the "mass of men whose very souls even now / Seem to need re-creating" (*Ring and the Book*, X. 1893–94). Eschewing simple attitudes, he conceives of triumph in terms of obstacles overcome and gives those obstacles their due. His habitual theme is man's impeded urge to bare his soul, his imperative but obstructed impulse to know himself.

4

"When a Soul Declares Itself": Varieties of Triumph

The most distinctive and, paradoxically, the most representative of Browning's poems is "Childe Roland." Despite the singularity of his wasteland adventure, the questing Roland is an Everyman, the summation of all Browning's monologists who seek and at the same time resist their particular truths. He rehearses the struggles of the unknown painter, the Bishop of St. Praxed's, Karshish, the Riccardi bride, her Duke, and all who solicit and fear an epiphany. Roland's mode of self-definition—he is one of "the Band" of "knights who to the Dark Tower's search [address] / Their steps" (ll. 40–41)—links him with characters such as Paracelsus and Andrea who profess one aim in life. His way of interpreting a meaningless landscape is a comment on the limits of introspection. More searchingly than any other poem in Browning's canon, "Childe Roland" examines the interaction of man's need for illusion and his willingness to confront a devastating truth.

The opening of the poem finds Roland doggedly, if not enthusiastically, pursuing his "world-wide wandering" (l. 19). Years of unsuccessful search have chastened him. Intensity has waned and only the fatigued recollection and habit of intensity are left; positive commitment has been reduced to mere relentlessness. Prepared for failure, he betrays all the signs of a man not yet beaten, but motivated by phantom selves. His hope has "dwindled into a ghost not fit to cope / With that obstreperous joy success would bring" (ll. 21–22), and his unacknowledged but real anxiety about the quest exaggerates all ambiguities. Roland's descriptions are, as Eugene Kintgen observes, "heightened imaginative renderings of what is actually seen, usually involving the attribution of malicious intent."[1] He warily suspects, for example, the integrity of the cripple who directs him into the "ominous tract which, all agree, / Hides the Dark Tower" (ll. 14–15); the man's look is disconcerting and makes even the surest fact ("all agree") a subject of painful doubt. If supposed certitudes provide occasions for such pause, how much more burdensome are the decisions Roland must make without received wisdom to guide him: paralysis seems almost inevitable. When he pauses "to throw backward a last view / O'er the safe road" (ll. 51–52), he finds that it has vanished utterly. This disappearance does not mean that his decision is right or wrong, but only that his acceptance of the cripple's counsel has closed off all other options; henceforth, he is deprived of even the illusory solace of the unknown painter and Andrea. His step into the path is suddenly irreversible; "I might go on; nought else remained to do" (l. 54).

In the context of the poem, the vanishing of the road constitutes one of the "unforeseen accidents of life"; such events, according to Browning, "throw one upon one's resources and show them for what they exactly are."[2] Roland, not surprisingly, has impressive resources. When the universe, with its mysterious guides and vanishing paths, does not disclose its purposes or encourage the belief that Roland is a consequential being, he projects meanings of his own. Using a logic that reality neither supplies nor corroborates, but that reinforces Roland's image of himself as questor, he peoples the landscape with opponents. He fancies himself first as the cripple's intended "victim" (l. 6) and then as an "estray" (l. 48) whom the leering sun and grey plain conspire to capture. A pledged rescuer and a slayer of monsters, he imagines a brute who "pashes" the vegetation (l. 71), a fiend who torments the sudden river into wrath (l. 113) and warriors who savagely trample the earth, but are themselves tortured victims whose frenzy approaches that of "toads in a poisoned tank, / Or wild cats in a red-hot iron cage" (ll. 131–32). He thinks of "the Turk" who pits galley slaves against one another (l. 137) and a viciously whimsical fool who "makes a thing and then mars it" (l. 148). The importance of these malicious tormentors is that they are so dreadfully necessary. The natural fantasies of one training for knighthood, they satisfy Roland's need to see the world in a particularly patterned way. They allow for the possibility of significant human action. They save him from the prospect of a blank, pointless universe and enable him to preserve his sense of role. Giants can be sought out; the void cannot.

Roland has more than one way of accommodating disturbing sights. Having no means to alter the prodigious woe of the "stiff blind horse" (l. 76), he recoils unsympathetically and imagines the beast "thrust out past service from the devil's stud!" (l. 78); "I never saw a brute I hated so; / He must be wicked to deserve such pain"(ll. 83–84). The idea of punishment is at least comprehensible, whereas that of extreme, irremediable and fortuitous suffering is not. But such rationality exacts its own price by reducing Roland to the status of an irrelevant witness. There is no role for him in this drama of retribution. Finding himself a functionless observer, Roland instinctively closes his eyes. And, like so many of Browning's speakers who feel their identity threatened, he resorts to introspection; "I shut my eyes and turned them on my heart" (l. 85). Because his vulnerability has to do with his role as questor, he bolsters himself with thoughts of the Band's shared mission. He defends himself against the demoralizing present by recalling the "old time" (l. 90). Accompanied formerly by Cuthbert of the golden curls and Giles "the soul of honour" (l. 97), Roland was once ardently secure of purpose, so now he coaxes "earlier, happier sights" (l. 87) out of the past. But this strategy proves subversive; his recollection is embittered by Cuthbert's disgrace and Giles's treachery. His chosen role is now both cosmically and primally endangered. So with desperate logic, Roland evades the enemy within and re-approaches the exterior; "Better this present than a past like that" (l. 103).

Roland returns to the "darkening path again" (l. 104) but with a growing fear of his own inconsequence. No man wants to know that "all is lost"; in *Easter-Day* (ll. 991–1003), the narrator goes so far as to ask for blind hope rather than such knowledge. Roland is not so blunt; he evades the sense of his contingency by subtle abstentions and refocusings of attention. His way of reacting to the landscape intensifies; his response still reflects his questor's orientation, but his careful

notice of the natural surfaces along the way suggests a strategic shifting
of interest. The idea of the quest still gives him a perspective on parti-
culars, but they begin to intrigue him unduly; he lingers psychically,
making concise but superfluous observations. There is an evasive
frenzy in his fascination with nature's textures, with wood, marsh, and
"stubbed ground" (1. 145). He catalogues and inventories:

> Bog, clay and rubble, sand and stark black dearth.

> Now blotches rankling, coloured gay and grim,
>   Now patches where some leanness of the soil's
>   Broke into moss or substances like boils.   (ll. 150–53).

Even the rhythm of these lines, with their tentative symmetry ("now
blotches," "now patches") quickly dispelled, suggests obsessiveness
and minute attention. There are good reasons for such intensity; it
justifies delay, postpones unwanted discoveries, and allows the luxury
of maintaining, while subtly suspending, his purposeful role. Roland's
dual reaction to the landscape bespeaks his self-division, what Kintgen
calls his "perversity of mind."[3] As questor, Roland still finds malevo-
lent tormentors behind the scenes, but he also identifies with the land
itself in all its helplessness. Nature, as he sees it, is in a condition that is
Biblically associated with the nadir of human history. The vegetation
seems to be marked by mysterious iniquity and in a state of eschatolog-
ical need. The thistles are in jealous discord:

> If there pushed any ragged thistle-stalk
>   Above its mates, the head was chopped; the bents
>   Were jealous else.   (ll. 67–69).

The "fell cirque" has the appearance of a battlefield:

>   what war did they wage,
>   Whose savage trample thus could pad the dank
>   Soil to a plash?   (ll. 129–31).

which suggests the violent rivalry of nations:

>   Mad brewage set to work
>   Their brains, no doubt, like galley-slaves the Turk
>   Pits for his pastime, Christians against Jews.   (ll. 136–36).

The very soil requires the purging of the final conflagration; and by articulating Nature's demand for apocalypse, Roland comes close to admitting his own helplessness:

> 'It nothing skills: I cannot help my case:
>   'T is the Last Judgment's fire must cure this place,
>   Calcine its clods and set my prisoners free.'   (ll. 64–66).

But Roland does not actually call for supernatural rescue; the elements of his identity—his twin views of himself as hero and victim —remain in suspension.

Were Roland to prove unfit, to succumb to premature failure, he could salvage the illusion of the quest structure. Because a missed goal is still a presumptive goal, his sense of personal orientation would survive. Roland as anti-hero would be a diminished but coherent type, a man whose defection would derive meaning from the quest itself. To surrender the goal without relinquishing the context for self-definition, "just to fail as they" (l. 41), is, therefore, a comforting temptation. But Roland does not seize the escape of defeat. This is his idiosyncratic strength, his peculiar fitness. Afraid of finally discovering his own purposelessness, he temporizes, but he does not wholly abandon the quest. Though the prospect of absolute fortuitousness is too terrible to embrace, he does not turn irrevocably away from it. He endures his ambivalence.

Eventually Roland reaches a point where he becomes aware that he is "just as far as ever from the end!" (l. 157). But he is prepared to push on and looks to the "great black bird" (l. 160) that brushes by him as a potential guide. Finding himself suddenly ringed by mountains, he concludes that there can be no farther "progress this way" (l. 172). As he confronts this dead end, he assumes, in keeping with his earlier intuitions of malicious tormentors, that this failure is the consequence of "some trick / Of mischief" (ll. 169–70). This refusal to blame himself is not, however, an existential declaration of independence. For Roland to suppose that he has been tricked into a particular *cul-de-sac* puts him on fairly comfortable terms with failure. His sense of aim in life remains intact and his questor's identity is preserved. To think that he is being hoaxed is to miss the cruelest hoax of all. But here, on the verge of premature failure and "in the very nick / Of giving up" (ll. 172–73), Roland makes a further discovery;

"Burningly it came on me all at once, / This was the place!" (ll. 175–76). What he almost mistakes for a dead end is The End. The quest proves pointless and the conclusion is the denial of the goal.

A brief look at "Cleon" will clarify the nature of Roland's epiphany. Cleon finds that his spiritual longing cannot be gratified and that there is some fault in existence *per se*. He concludes with "profound discouragement" that "life's inadequate to joy" (l. 249). He even raises, if only to dismiss, the notion that Zeus maliciously intends for man to strive and despair. Cleon's analysis bears on Roland's situation. When a questor endures his anxieties and marches relentlessly in pursuit of a chosen goal, his inability to find it, his reaching of dead ends, may be attributable to several causes; and the most disturbing possibilities are precisely those raised by Cleon. The universe may be hostile to man or it may be radically unsuited to his needs. The latter more shattering discovery is the one that quitters never actually make. "Master Hugues of Saxe-Gotha" is relevant here, too. The organist confronts one of the Master's "mountainous fugues" (l. 4). He assumes that the piece, with its obfuscating musical phrases, must be an expression of the master's "moral of Life" (l. 106). Unwilling to consider the possibility of meaninglessness, he falls victim to what A. O. Lovejoy calls "metaphysical pathos"; the organist loves the music for its "sheer obscurity, the loveliness of the incomprehensible."[4] He affirms without warrant, and contrary to his own experience, that "hard number twelve" (l. 33) does mean something; "Who thinks Hugues wrote for the deaf / Proved a mere mountain in labour?" (ll. 126–27). Browning rewards such willfully unexamined trust by plunging the organist into darkness. Roland, however, faces the prospect that his quest is meaningless and that failure is a cosmic inevitability. He discovers that he has committed and wasted himself in a "rash pursuit of aims / That life affords not" (*Paracelsus* I. 94–95). A host of commentators have speculated what Roland's particular aim might be,[5] but its precise nature is of far less interest than the confrontation with its non-existence.

Roland's epiphany is pure contradiction; he discovers what he does not wholly want to discover. His success is the acknowledgment that there is no success. His search leads to the recognition that searches are futile. This hard-won awareness constitutes a metaphysical certitude that validates the structure it invalidates. The loss of externally conferred meaning is in itself a kind of meaning.[6] Browning's achievement is that he incorporates these paradoxes in a concrete symbol of denial:

> What in the midst lay but the Tower itself?
>> The round squat turret, blind as the fool's heart,
>> Built of brown stone, without a counterpart
> In the whole world.   (ll. 181–184).

Roland's epiphany, as is customary in Browning's poetry, is represented as an unforeseen event. The truth is sprung like a trap; revelation sounds like a "click" (l. 173); and he comes upon the tower unawares: "Dotard, a-dozing at the very nonce, / After a life spent training for the sight!" (ll. 179–80). What Roland discovers is that he is located in the center of an annihilating context: "The hills, like giants at hunting, lay, / Chin upon hand, to see the game at bay" (ll. 190–91). All his intuitions of cruel giants are realized and transformed, for Roland finds himself ambushed by inanity. To reach the Tower is to be nullified, and the moment of discovery is linked with death and betrayal:

>> The tempest's mocking elf
> Points to the shipman thus the unseen shelf
>> He strikes on, only when the timbers start.   (ll. 184–86).

This is the ultimate joke; Roland faces the goal that is the annihilation of the goal-seeking identity.

The entire cosmos takes part in the act of revelation. The universe is transformed and the knight's senses are bombarded with the stunning truth:

> Not see? because of night perhaps?—why, day
>> Came back again for that!   (ll. 187–88).

> Not hear? when noise was everywhere! it tolled
>> Increasing like a bell.   (ll. 193–94).

The scene has the quality of the Last Judgment; even the lost and failed members of the Band reappear in a sheet of apocalyptic fire. They evaded until physical death the obliteration of self that Roland now confronts. His is a more terrible form of the unique but universal experience of unmeaning; thus it is chastening but exhilarating to have the Band as witness:

> There they stood, ranged along the hill-sides, met
> > To view the last of me, a living frame
> > For one more picture! in a sheet of flame
> I saw them and I knew them all.   (ll. 199–202).

Roland feels strangely unafraid now that he is released from the subversive anxiety of the quest. Enclosure and entrapment bring almost a kind of relief, for the act of pursuit never wholly marshalled his energies; orientation did not bestow a welcome inevitability. Having discovered the terrible truth, he is suddenly at peace with himself; the inner struggle, the simultaneous striving and resisting, is now abated, irrelevant. The loss of an end-directed identity—and this is Browning's great discovery—leaves Roland in possession of himself. He is capable of coherent gesture. When Roland lifts the slug–horn, he says, in effect, "I am I, though utterly and irrevocably bereft of purpose." The significance of Roland's experience is his changing reaction to the quest: his projections, his misperceptions and final epiphany. By confronting the spectre of ultimate meaninglessness, Roland establishes his essential autonomy. The discovery that he is an aimless wanderer who has mistaken himself for a questor does not make him a failure. On the contrary, to recognize projection as projection is to be freed of it as delusion—and that is Roland's triumph.

Roland's march through his nightmarishly unstable landscape apparently satisfies his creator's need, for Browning does not write this way again; the style of the poem, which Arthur Symons aptly characterized as "romantic realism," is a singular achievement.[7] This is not to say, however, that Roland's experience is unique. His emotions are shared by other of Browning's characters, and some undergo analogous, if less surreal, experiences of annihilation. John, for example, in "A Death in the Desert," is forced by ordinary mortality to relinquish his temporal role. In his poem as in Roland's, Browning undermines his hero's identity in order to affirm the independence of the essential self. According to the narrator, the apostle is well beyond the reach of sensory stimulation when his friends try to rouse him. Impervious to sunlight, wine, perfume, the cooling of his forehead, or the chafing of his hands, he responds only to the repetition of Christ's words "I am the Resurrection and the Life" (l. 64). Even then, like the posthumous Lazarus, he is bewildered by his return to life. "Superficial" truths (l. 113), including his own identity, temporarily elude him. This blurriness about his person is more than a matter of dying confusion; it is the dramatic embodiment of Browning's fully serious hypothesis about levels of being. John believes that he has withdrawn from his corporeal self to an interior core:

> So is myself withdrawn into my depths,
> The soul retreated from the perished brain
> Whence it was wont to feel and use the world
> Through these dull members, done with long ago.
>
> (ll. 76–79);

and he makes an astonishing claim: "Yet I myself remain; I feel myself: / And there is nothing lost" (ll. 80–81). Like Roland at the Dark Tower, the disciple is essentially self-possessed; he has attained to the level of the "last soul" (l. 95) described in the "glossa of Theotypas" (l. 104):

> This is the doctrine he was wont to teach,
> How divers persons witness in each man,
> Three souls which make up one soul: first, to wit,
> A soul of each and all the bodily parts,
> Seated therein, which works, and is what Does,
> And has the use of earth, and ends the man
> Downward: but, tending upward for advice,
> Grows into, and again is grown into
> By the next soul, which, seated in the brain,
> Useth the first with its collected use,
> And feeleth, thinketh, willeth,—is what Knows:
> Which, duly tending upward in its turn,
> Grows into, and again is grown into
> By the last soul, that uses both the first,
> Subsisting whether they assist or no,
> And, constituting man's self, is what Is—   (ll. 82–97).

The reader need not worry about whether this doctrine of subsistent being is John's or pseudo-John's or wonder about the identity of the editor who inserts Theotypas' comment. Browning plainly attributes to all three a belief in the autonomy of the authentic self. There is an interior John distinct from "your brother" (l. 116) and from all the incidentals of his own biography.

Once revived, John generalizes from his personal estrangement to that of men in the future; his severance from who he is and where he is in time provokes the thought of his inevitable separation from succeeding generations. John's self-alienation finds expression in an imagined expedition through space and time. Wandering in unseen realms, he finds "unborn people in strange lands" (l. 194) who are uncertain whether he ever actually existed. Fully cognizant that he is the last eye-witness of Christ, he wonders, "How will it be when none more saith 'I saw'?" (l. 133). He ponders the future of Christianity and the caution of coming generations who will want the facts about John before they accept his teachings about Christ; "Was John at all, and did he say he saw? / Assure us, ere we ask what he might see!" (ll. 196–97). (John's attendant, supposedly Pamphylax, asserts that confusion about John already exists and that this account is intended, in part, to confirm the apostle's death.) John's ensuing remarks suggest, however, that the temporal distance which separates men from him and from Christ is not a matter of increased deprivation. The passage of time can be an advantage, a means of release from the local and contingent. John affirms that his sense of Christ's life is clearer for such distance:

> Much that at first, in deed or word,
> Lay simply and sufficiently exposed,
> Had grown . . .
> Of new significance.   (ll. 168–73).

The past articulates "fresh result" (l. 173) because the mature apostle himself brings a "new significance" to it:

> My soul was grown to match,
> Fed through such years, familiar with such light,
> Guarded and guided still to see and speak.   (ll. 171–72).

The ripened soul is the means of discovery. As the apostle becomes more aware of his essential self, his superficial identity is less a barrier; the "years assist" (1. 201) in wearing away "the thickness" (1. 202) of youth so that the soul lies "bare to the universal prick of light" (1. 205).

Such wearing away is not easy or automatic and John does not underestimate the "burthen for late days" (1. 337). Knowing that the future believer faces an ongoing ordeal of historical consciousness, he anticipates the complaint that belief "had been easier once" (1. 299). He develops a theory of faith that turns out, upon examination, to be a variation on Browning's theme of impediment. The individual soul defines itself in part by the barriers it overcomes. Because obstacles are a means for "keeping the soul's prowess possible" (1. 269), chronically aggravated doubt about Christ serves a necessary moral function. John asserts simply that "to test man, the proofs shift" (1. 295). Commitment will always be possible because the context will always be unprecedented. New necessities will forever beget new possibilities. The condition of ever-renewed incertitude is similar to that in "Childe Roland." Believing in his quest and even knowing the direction of the Tower, Roland nevertheless has to confront the cripple's malice and determine independently whether to follow his guidance. It is by bearing the burden of difficult personal decisions and by living with chronically refreshed anxiety that he proves himself fit. Religious belief, in John's view, is an analogous kind of fitness. The individual, moreover, who longs for an unattainable degree of certitude risks atrophy. He may never reach the moment of choice and never get on with the business of being a Christian. John anticipates this spiritual malady and urges future generations to "Use [faith] and forthwith, or die!" (1. 481). The self-division of the disbelieving-believer must be endured; the severance from truth must be the basis for living faith.

John's dying words supposedly survive because Pamphylax dictated his account to Phoebas to which several editors then contributed their labors. This collective effort makes "A Death in the Desert," with its various accretions, something more than a simple monologue. The poem represents a stage in the transmission of a text. The editor's concern with the condition of his source—"It . . . / Hath three skins glued together, is all Greek" (ll. 2–3)—his explicit affirmation of belief, his inclusion of Theotypas' gloss, and the concluding segments by and about other readers indicate that this document exists as part of a continuum. The preservation of John's speech is meant to provide proof of his existence and to counteract the doubts he anticipates. But the edited condition of the text, not to mention some of its subtle confusions, calls attention to its status as a historied and composite artifact. The document *per se* is an obstacle to belief. It elicits a response manifestly at odds with the transcribers' intentions and creates rather than forestalls doubts.

As DeVane and others have shown, Browning has the new forms of Biblical criticism in mind, those currently jeopardizing the authority of Scripture.[8] And his poem suggests that there is a crucial difference between a text and its content. This dichotomy, one should add, is in keeping with Browning's personal habits. There is abundant proof of his physical irreverence towards what he clearly regarded as important books and papers. His first copy of Shelley's poetry, for example, the *Miscellaneous Poems* of 1826, is notoriously mutilated[9] and though the *Old Yellow Book* is safely housed at Balliol College, Oxford, the narrator of *The Ring and the Book* casually tosses it about (I. 33–35). Even the proof copy of Browning's own poems gives evidence of abuse; the corrections in *Dramatis Personae* are inked in over erasures with "somewhat illegible results."[10] Browning's insensitivity to texts as objects is not in itself important. But the distinction he apparently makes between books and the truths they convey replicates the difference he perceives between the presiding and essential selves. Whether Browning refutes or joins the higher critics, his method of dealing with them is consistent with his view of human nature.[11] He believes in the layering of selves and of truths. The essence of a text, like the core of being, exists in a way and at a level that is distinguishable from its surface. If disestablishing an identity puts one in contact with the authentic self, then criticizing a text may be a way of reaching its inner truth. Alienation from the non-essential is an opportunity for verification; and documents, like selves, may yield up a revelation when they are discredited.

Browning has many ways of discussing the process of self-disclosure. In "Childe Roland" the metaphor is annihilation while for John it is wearing away. For Browning's converts, the manifestation of the true self involves rejection or destruction. But in all cases

Browning's language suggests that the true self is obscured; revelation occurs only with the removal of some barrier. This theme is the basis of Browning's love poetry as well. The intimacy between two people is yet another way for him to think about access to the self. Commitment, in his view, is an act of self-realization. In choosing his beloved, the individual enacts possibilities that would otherwise remain unlived; his surrender, like the convert's confession or John's maturing, is a means of soul-baring.

Browning knows that the process of falling in love may be gradual, but in "By the Fire-side" he imagines the lovers' culminating acknowledgment as the work of a moment.[12] Communication is definitive, portentous, and, because the speaker is so painfully inhibited—"convulsed to really speak," (l. 164)—nearly accidental. The truth must be expressed spontaneously or not at all; and, as with Browning's converts, the unforeseen nature of the episode is the mark of its authenticity. Sentimentalists relish the fragile momentousness of the occasion; "Oh, the little more, and how much it is! / And the little less, and what worlds away!" (ll. 191–92). Thomas Hardy found it painful and quoted the second line in *Tess of the d'Urbervilles* to summarize Angel Clare's chilling meditation on "the harrowing contingencies of human experience, the unexpectedness of things."[13] But the critic should notice that Browning's handling of the scene is relevant to his interpretation of other psychological crises. The lover is extraordinarily passive; he, like Aprile, seems perfectly capable of neglecting the means of securing what he so ardently desires. He has apparently no confidence that a declaration of love will do anything more than endanger a friendship. Like the poet in *Pauline*, helplessly in doubt of his own powers, he conjures up an image of involuntary relief. The fall of a leaf, when compared with the intervention of a Perseus, is probably the least convincing right-angled event in all of Browning's poetry, but it serves. The timid lover fancies that the communication he cannot effect will be somehow accomplished, like the fortuitous bestowal of a grace:

> a last leaf—fear to touch!
>
> Yet should it unfasten itself and fall
>   Eddying down till it find your face
> At some slight wind—best chance of all! (ll. 210–13).

The one who does the conferring is the lady, and the psychological impediments that might possibly have hindered her are acknowledged. Had she been reluctant, then "still had stood the screen" between them (l. 196). They might have remained like the "Two in the Campagna," isolated, uncommitted, and aware only of "infinite passion, and the pain / Of finite hearts that yearn" (ll. 59–60). They might, like the lovers in "Youth and Art," have had to lament, "This could but have happened once, / And we missed it, lost it forever" (ll. 67–68). But mute declarations *are* made and they become "mixed at last / In spite of the mortal screen" (ll. 234–35) The successful overcoming of inhibition is further emphasized by reference to a "bar" that is "broken between / Life and life" (ll. 233–34). This association of images is not new to Browning; it appears in his first letter to Elizabeth:

> Do you know I was once not very far from seeing—really seeing you? Mr. Kenyon said to me one morning "Would you like to see Miss Barrett?"—then he went to announce me,—then he returned. .you were too unwell—and now it is years ago—and I feel as at some untoward passage in my travels—as if I had been close, so close, to some world's-wonder in chapel or crypt, only a screen to push and I might have entered, but there was some slight. .so it now seems. .slight and just sufficient bar to admission.[14]

The world knows how Robert and Elizabeth dealt with their bar, but the removal effected by the lovers in "By the Fire-side" warrants further comment. Browning resorts to a favorite technique to describe the process, one he also uses in "Saul." After David's visionary experience, the entire cosmos seems to take tumultuous part in his rapture. The prophet who speaks of transcendence as a literal elevation feels sustained amid chaos by God's own hand:

> I fainted not
> For the Hand still impelled me at once and supported, suppressed
> All the tumult, and quenched it with quiet, and holy behest,
> Till the rapture was shut in itself, and the earth sank to rest.
>
> (ll. 320–23).

But what David construes as miracle strikes the reader as a psychological symbol. The outbreak and suppression of stellar turbulence externalize the process of post-apocalyptic mediation. Nature enacts a drama that corresponds to David's experience of vision and assimilation. There is no precipitous falling off in this passage, but a necessary and successful modulation. A drama of the same sort, though less spectacular, occurs in "By the Fire-side." The forest seems to the lover to be restlessly silent as if it labored to deliver some oppressive message, "It must get rid of what it knows, / Its bosom does so heave" (ll. 159–60). Preoccupied by the struggle with his own inhibition, he finds sign of some "trouble" (l. 190) in the motion of lights and shadows. With the lovers' revelation, however, all becomes placid:

> The water slips o'er stock and stone;
> The West is tender, hardly bright;
> How grey at once is the evening grown—
> One star, its chrysolite! (ll. 182–85).

The lover's relief seems matched by a change in his forest surroundings, "Their work was done. . . / They relapsed to their ancient mood" (ll. 239–40). The lover's achievement, like David's, is a miracle of self-revelation; and in these passages both man and nature experience the "quiet and holy" euphoria of realization.

"That moment's feat" is as consequential as the response to a religious calling; the speaker is "named and known" by it (l. 251). He feels, as Jacob Korg remarks,

> not that he is one with nature, but that his intuitions have been confirmed by something distinct from himself, that his life and the alien life of the external world have intersected in a rare, miraculous meeting.[15]

The lover's sense of the setting, in other words, associates the expression of human love with supernatural revelation and the declaration of one's identity with epiphany.

Except for a handful of speakers, Browning's characters are rarely heard from once they accept their commitments. "By the Fire-side" is somewhat unusual in this regard, for the narrator speaks of "an age so blest that, by its side, / Youth seems the waste instead" (ll. 124–25). He loves the woman of his choice and experiences the kind of life that Norbert, the poor hero of "In a Balcony," can only anticipate:

> I look to a long life
> To decompose this minute, prove its worth.
> 'T is the sparks' long succession one by one
> Shall show you, in the end, what fire was crammed
> In that mere stone you struck;   (ll. 642–46).

As the narrator explores the significance of his married love, it becomes evident that his motive is similar to the convert's impulse to bear witness or the renewed artist's breaking of silence. The passing from a state of disbelief, inhibition or isolation virtually requires confession; and the desire to affirm one's identity becomes imperative even for a lover.

The husband's meditation is more than remembrance of things past; musing how he shall spend "life's November" (1. 5), he anticipates other such meditations by the fire. He predicts future recollections of the past, particularly of the forest episode, which he proceeds to narrate in the present tense; the past within the future is thus brought into the present. This same chronology occurs in Browning's love letters. On one occasion, for example, he imagines for Elizabeth that "we are married, . . . and I am asking you, '*Were you not* to me, in that dim beginning of 1846, . . .the good I chose from all the possible gifts of God on this earth. . . ?'"[16] In the poem, the narrator complicates the chronology still further by noticing, within the historical present of the forest episode, that there are fresh toadstools along the path. He fancies their previous twenty-four hours of growth:

> The rose-flesh mushrooms, undivulged
> Last evening—nay, in to-day's first dew
> Yon sudden coral nipple bulged,
> Where a freaked fawn-coloured flaky crew
> Of toadstools peep indulged.   (ll. 61–65).[17]

This curious nesting of temporal sequences has the effect of collapsing time and subduing an entire life to the unifying power of the lovers' moment of assent.

As the narrator's imagination returns to the Alpine gorge, certain distinctions become irrelevant and he finds himself, in more ways than one, standing again "in the heart of things" (l. 36). Just as all time is unified by this moment, so too the details of the remembered scene suggest the interconnectedness of all space. Things apparently remote are brought into imagined proximity; the stream running through the woods, "the thread of water single and slim" (l. 39), may feed the lake in the valley below. And in the "evening-glow" (l.43) of their lofty vantage point, the lovers see where the "Alp meets heaven in snow" (l. 45). The empty chapel stimulates, not a meditation on isolation and decay, but thoughts of the "festa-day" when the "dozen folk" come from their "scattered homes" and gather "within that precinct small" (ll. 78–79). Even the barriers between animate and inanimate break down as the speaker notices, and reverses, the subtly mimetic relationship of the moth and its environment:

> A path is kept. . .
> By the boulder-stones where lichens mock
> The marks on a moth.   (ll. 47–49).

This collapsing of distinctions and telescoping of time and space culminate in the exclamation, "Oh moment, one and infinite!" (l. 181).

The memory of this time transcending experience gives rise to thoughts of the apocalyptic end of all time "when earth breaks up and heaven expands" (l. 133). During the moment in the woods, the focus of life becomes so apparent—everything "tends to some moment's product thus" (l. 243)—that life seems "complete" (l. 253). The lover's personal history is so coherent that he feels himself profoundly in relation to what Frank Kermode calls the history of history itself. The orientation of his own life is so clear that he has a tranquil and integrated sense of ending.[18] To put the matter another way, the power that revives the past anticipates the future as well, and here, as in "Saul," introspection borders on prophecy. The narrator fancies that he shall welcome death and wonders about the life of lovers when "The great Word . . . makes all things new" (l. 132). He does not think their love will suffer change. His wife has always been a means of revelation, and he imagines her continuing this function in eternity. She will "see and make me see . . . / New depths of the divine!" (ll. 139–40).

In "One Word More" Browning again treats the theme of lovers' mutual disclosure and suggests, as he does in *Pauline*, the similarity of human and divine epiphanies. The lady in the earlier poem is a very vague figure but apparently capable of influence. Crediting her with his restoration, the lover expresses gratitude in lines that echo Shelley's "Hymn to Intellectual Beauty":

> when I lost all hope of such a change,
> Suddenly beauty rose on me again,
> No less I make an end in perfect joy,
> For I, who thus again was visited,
> Shall doubt not many another bliss awaits.   (ll. 1005–9).[19]

The experience of Pauline's love is thus hinted to be as effective as a supernatural visitation. Browning develops this comparison in "One Word More" using the image of lunar manifestation. The phases of the moon as it waxes and wanes to "a piece of her old self impoverished" (l. 153) are publicly observed phenomena. Every "herdsman, huntsman, steersman" (l. 163) may watch her transfiguration. But in the tale of Endymion, the moon blesses a chosen individual by turning "a new side to her mortal" (l. 161). The myth has special application, for even "the meanest" of men (l. 184) "boasts two soul-sides" (l. 185) and may, like the deity, reveal a new side to the woman he loves. With this stroke, Browning makes an opportunity of self-division. The bright side, the presiding self by which the world identifies an individual, hides another authentic surface. This concealment, ordinarily regarded as lamentable, is cause for celebration. The obscure self, so repressed and difficult of access is, for this very reason, a precious mystery and its disclosure an almost supernatural event.

Because the moon is a goddess in the "old sweet mythos" (l. 160), the tale applies more readily to a woman's revelation, and Browning makes direct reference to Elizabeth. Calling her "my moon of poets" (l. 188), he takes pride in her public brilliance;

> that's the world's side, there's the wonder,
> Thus they see you, praise you, think they know you!
> There, in turn I stand with them and praise you—
>
> (ll. 189–91).

But this kind of praise is almost fraudulent; to admire her as if he stood on "the world's side" (l. 189) is to respond uncharacteristically, "out of my own self, I dare to phrase it" (l. 192). It is only her private self that engages his private self and he hastens to view her

> other side, the novel
> Silent silver lights and darks undreamed of,
> Where I hush and bless myself with silence.   (ll. 195–97).

A man who does not feel similarly blessed by his beloved might find her visibility in the world unsettling, and Browning works several variations on the theme. The Duke of Ferrara resents that his lady "liked whate'er / She looked on, and her looks went everywhere" (ll. 23–24), while Andrea del Sarto praises his beautiful Lucrezia as "My face, my moon, my everybody's moon, / Which everybody looks on and calls his" (ll. 29–30), but concludes with gradual anticlimax and telling omission, "And, I suppose, is looked on by in turn, / While she looks—no one's" (ll. 31–32).

With characteristic density, Browning alludes in "One Word More" to mythical, Biblical and natural epiphanies to suggest the awesome seriousness of receiving a soul's revelation. He stresses Endymion's altered perception and the anxiety with which this "moonstruck mortal" (l. 166) watches the next moonrise. Anticipation of her awful loveliness inspires both rapture and fear; she is as dreadful as the destructive forces in nature;

> like some portent of an iceberg
> Swimming full upon the ship it founders,
> Hungry with huge teeth of splintered crystals.   (ll. 169–71).

The moon cannot, without blasphemy, be identified with Yahweh, but her beauty is safely comparable to that of the jeweled pavement on which he appears to his prophets:

> Proves she as the paved work of a sapphire
> Seen by Moses when he climbed the mountain?
> Moses, Aaron, Nadab, and Abihu
> Climbed and saw the very God, the Highest
> Stand upon the paved work of a sapphire.   (ll. 172–76).

In "One Word More" and "By the Fire-side" the male speaker's gratitude is stressed, and Browning's point is that an individual who loves accomplishes a revelation; his "soul declares itself" ("By the Fire-side" l. 244). The emotion he spends on another releases something essential in his nature. In loving he achieves what many of Browning's characters, using as many metaphors, desire. He is in touch with his central self "distinct from all its qualities" (*Pauline*, l. 270); he discovers his "spirit's true endowments" ("Cristina" l. 20); he emits a "vindicating ray" ("Flight of the Duchess," l. 604), a "bright escape / Of soul" ("Two Poets of Croisic" ll. 346–7). His triumph counteracts Browning's often expressed fear that the genuine self may be virtually unreachable. The unknown painter, the Bishop of St. Praxed's, and Sludge may seem irremediably inauthentic, but the lovers of "By the Fire-side" and "One Word More" achieve genuine self-knowledge. Intense passion confers a sense of integrity; the energies of the soul are marshalled in a way that feels inevitable and right. The lover, moreover, is known by the beloved, not simply in his oriented unity, but in all his chaotic multiplicity. This is perhaps the most personally gratifying hypothesis in Browning's metaphysic of love. In their early correspondence, Robert reminds Elizabeth that she knows "nothing" of him. He tries to tell her that "for every poor speck of a Vesuvius or a Stromboli in my microcosm there are huge layers of ice and pits of black cold water."[20] But the "grand" and embarrassed simile collapses and he concludes with the distressed admission that he is "utterly unused, of these late years particularly to dream of communicating anything about that to another person." His bewilderment is akin to that of his own early artists, particularly Sordello who longs to exhibit all his soul's power but finds himself

> footing a delusive round,
> Remote as ever from the self-display
> He meant to compass.   (II. 650–52).

In "One Word More" Browning admits the fear that he can never "all-express" himself (l. 111). But he now believes that love accomplishes what art only approximates, and he joyfully tells Elizabeth "you know me" (l. 144). Lovers, he affirms, can comprehend one another's innermost selves. Such knowledge echoes the psalmist's grateful acknowledgment of God' omniscience:

O Lord, thou hast searched me, and known me . . . thou understandest my thought afar off . . . For there is not a word in my tongue but, lo, O Lord, thou knowest it altogether.   (Psalm 139:1–4).

This kind of intimacy is also achieved by Pompilia and Caponsacchi in *The Ring and the Book*. In their first completely nonverbal encounter at the theater, the priest sees into Pompilia's soul and discovers her essential goodness. This knowledge bestows a kind of prophetic power; reality becomes so transparent for him that even Guido's forged love letters cannot impugn Pompilia's innocence:

> Pompilia spoke, and I at once received,
> Accepted my own fact, my miracle
> Self-authorized and self-explained.   (VI. 918–20).

Pompilia, too, sees through Guido's attempt to stage-manage their mutual misrecognition:

>   As I
> Recognized her, at potency of truth,
> So she, by the crystalline soul, knew me,
> Never mistook the signs.   (VI. 931–34).

There are numerous such episodes in Browning's poetry; indeed, they recur with the frequency of a personal myth. The mode of communication is mysterious, but two souls, nonetheless, become reciprocally accessible. In "Count Gismond" the knight intuits the lady's innocence while she "at first view" (l. 69) knows him for her defender; in "The Italian in England" the patriot is persuaded "at first sight of her eyes" (l. 63) of the peasant woman's loyalty; and in "The Flight of the Duchess" the huntsman narrator attempts to explain how he and the Duchess understood each other. He is no metaphysician, but his naive effort is suggestive:

> As for finding what she wanted,
> You know God Almighty granted
> Such little signs should serve wild creatures
> To tell one another all their desires,
> So that each knows what his friend requires.   (ll. 725–29).

Reciprocal understanding is as intuitive as self-understanding. If Browning seems unrealistically insistent on non-verbal communication in these poems, it is because he knows how easily language distorts. The Italian, for example, plans to act like any of a number of Browning's manipulative speakers and prepares a lie that cannot "fail / Persuade a peasant of its truth" (ll. 52–53). Yet he and the woman come to an understanding *before* he attempts to control how she perceives him. Recognition precedes and happily forestalls deception. Browning knows that silence is often cowardly—witness all his silent poets—but because speech is nearly as often a form of concealment, he sometimes conceives of silence as an instrument of revelation. He can imagine a "marriage of true minds" in which thoughts replace words, a unity of souls which eliminates the possibility of verbal distortion:

> if I think but deep enough,
> You are wont to answer, prompt as rhyme;
> And you, too, find without rebuff
> Response your soul seeks many a time
> Piercing its fine flesh-stuff.   ("By the Fire-side," ll. 116–20).

The consequence of such "piercing" is the theme of Caponsacchi's monologue. His means of defending Pompilia is to explain what it meant to see into her soul and how, by knowing her, he came to know himself. His monologue represents a remarkable development of a theme presented tentatively in "Cristina." This early poem suggests that the focusing of emotion can alter one's self-perception. It takes only a glance for the lady to "discover / All her soul" (ll. 4–5) to the poem's speaker; and although it is impossible to unravel an exact sequence of cause and effect, the knowledge of the lady gives the speaker a new clarity about himself. He is suddenly sure which "poor impulse" (l. 29) is to be pursued as "the sole work of a life-time" (l. 31). He speaks of the event as one of life's "moments,"

> When the spirit's true endowments
> Stand out plainly from its false ones,
> And apprise it if pursuing
> Or the right way or the wrong way,
> To its triumph or undoing.   (ll. 20–24).

If he were pursuing the "wrong way," the lady's glance would, he implies, effect his conversion. The difficulty with "Cristina" is that the speaker is so uncourtly, it seems more than likely he has misread the lady's look. He may, like Caliban or the lover in "Misconceptions," have misconstrued an epiphany. But Caponsacchi is more reliable than Cristina's admirer, and his belief in a connection between knowledge of Pompilia and knowledge of himself is convincing.

Caponsacchi challenges his judges to compare the factual outlines as well as the emotional coloring of this and his earlier testimony. He warns them that his sense of the past is informed by recent and imminent events:

> —turn and see
> If, by one jot or tittle, I vary now!
> I' the colour the tale takes, there's change perhaps;
> 'T is natural, since the sky is different,
> Eclipse in the air now; Still, the outline stays.   (VI. 1644–48).

This second court presentation incorporates the same data, the identical set of episodes, but it is also a dynamically fresh act of perception. Caponsacchi, like John in "A Death in the Desert," knows that facts which once seemed "sufficiently exposed" can acquire "new significance" ("Death," ll. 169, 173). The shock of Pompilia's murder makes the priest see his life in patterned ways, and, like many of Browning's speakers, he draws on the idea of his calling to give shape to his confession.[21] He begins by admitting his callow attitude towards his ordination and his vague expectation of instantaneous passage into some "other life":

> I must read the vows,
> Declare the world renounced and undertake
> To become priest and leave probation,—leap
> Over the ledge into the other life.   (VI. 262–65).

He admits, too, a complete insincerity about the keeping of vows. But this compromise of his priestly vocation is exposed, its moral worth retrospectively adjusted, by his authentic response to Pompilia's summons. Because of her, he now regards his ordination as a squandered opportunity for commitment and transformation. It was a fraudulent initiation, an almost frolicsome and unimpeded "leap" that went nowhere. He expands on his balky attitude towards the vows and remembers his religious superior's obliging assurances about the historical irrelevance of self-sacrifice. The Bishop, like Blougram, believes that the Church can accommodate the world; he authorizes a life of impersonation and sanctions the charade whereby Caponsacchi calls himself a priest of God and yet lives the life of a courtier. Ordination on such terms is a form of self-betrayal. It reduces his vocation to an institutional alliance having much to do with ecclesiastical preferment, but little with holiness. The years of this devitalized priesthood are dismissed in three brisk lines:

> Well, after three or four years of this life,
> In prosecution of my calling, I
> Found myself at the theatre one night.   (VI. 393–95).

This event at the theatre has the force of a true ordination. Pompilia teaches Caponsacchi that he is pursuing "the wrong way" ("Cristina" l. 23). Her "beautiful sad strange smile" (VI. 412) exerts an immediate and continuing pressure. She is what Palma would call an "out-soul" (*Sordello* III, 320), a force Sordello describes in terms of moon and tide:

> A soul . . . above his soul
> Power to uplift his power,—such moon's control
> Over such sea-depths.   (VI. 41–43).

The metaphor is apt, for Pompilia exercises her "moon's control" at a distance. Before Caponsacchi ever speaks to her, his imagination is captivated by images of illumination, transformation, and miracle. He goes, soon after the evening at the theater, to the Duomo to

> watch the day's last gleam outside
> Turn, as into a skirt of God's own robe,
> Those lancet-windows' jewelled miracle.   (VI. 460–62).

More important still, the thought of Pompilia stimulates a new concern with himself. In thinking "how utterly dissociated" he is "from the sad strange wife of Guido" (VI. 492, 93), Caponsacchi comes to a realization of his own self-severance; he sees, for the first time, how arbitrarily he has repressed his better self. He discovers a "whole store of strengths / Eating into [his] heart, which [crave] employ" (VI. 495–96). This single silent contact with Pompilia makes him suddenly impatient with his non-genuineness; "Beset and pressed hard by some novel thoughts" (VI. 476), he confronts his spiritual inadequacy:

> thinking how my life
> Had shaken under me,—broke short indeed
> And showed a gap, 'twixt what is, what should be,—
> And into what abysm the soul may slip,
> Leave aspiration here, achievement there. (VI. 485–89).

Caponsacchi's recognition of the disparity between aspiration and enacted existence replicates the crises of Pauline's poet, Andrea del Sarto, and numerous other monologists. Such an epiphany can paralyze, but in Caponsacchi's case the discovery of his frivolous and humiliating inconsequence amounts to a conversion. "The look o' the lady" (VI. 1012) puts him in touch with his ideal self and reveals the "right way"; he knows, henceforth, that "There [is] no duty patent in the world / Like daring try be good and true myself" (VI. 1818–19). Plagued by the sense of his own fraudulence, he resolves to go to Rome and "look into [his] heart a little" (VI. 481). And when the worldly bishop, curious about the change in Caponsacchi, asks if he is "turning Molinist" (VI. 473), the priest replies, "Sir, what if I turned Christian?" (VI. 474).

The artists and lovers in Browning's poetry have similar opportunities and related kinds of failures. He imagines relationships that validate, as in Caponsacchi's monologue, or alienate, as in "Andrea del Sarto," the lover's innermost being. And what is true about attachments to others is also true of objects. A man's relations with phenomena may be revealing, as in "Saul," or merely obsessive, as in "The Bishop Orders his Tomb." He can attend to externals as a means of discovery or reduce them to simple paraphernalia. The true artist, like the genuine lover, must overcome internal barriers; he, too, faces obstacles which preclude full commitment. There are clear affinities between the speaker of "By the Fire-side," for example, and Fra Lippo Lippi. The monk, like the hesitant lover, is a man divided. Though it is tempting to see Lippo as a man oppressed, it would be a serious misreading of the poem to blame the Carmelites, the Medici, or even the times for Lippo's difficulties. He depends, it is true, upon patrons who want "saints and saints / And saints again" (ll. 48–49), but the forces that frustrate Lippo are psychological, not socio-economic.[22] His worry about the value of "perishable clay" (l. 180) threatens his aesthetic attachment to the world.

The immediate occasion for Brother Lippo's monologue is his capture by the night watch. He responds to their rough handling and torches with the Florentine equivalent of name, rank, serial number, and a vociferous "Zooks, what's to blame?" (l. 3). His mode is alternately threatening, "Remember and tell me, the day you're hanged, / How you affected such a gullet's-gripe" (ll. 19–20), and placating, "Drink out this quarter-florin to the health / Of the munificent House that harbours me" (ll. 28–29).[23] These two modes are rhetorical strategies for manipulating the soldiers, but this belligerency and bribery also reflect the serious ambivalence of Lippo's attitude towards himself. He does not need to defend his night's adventure to the soldiers; his escapade at the "alley's end / Where sportive ladies leave their doors ajar" (ll. 5–6) is obvious enough. He needs to apologize, in the true sense of that word, for offenses these "hangdogs" could not possibly comprehend. It is not his accidental capture, but a coincidence of gesture, that sets Lippo talking seriously to himself. When the captain of the guard expresses his disapproval, his nod— "you shake your head" (l. 76)—recalls the aesthetic disapprobation of the learned Carmelites: "The heads shake still—It's art's decline, my son! / You're not of the true painters, great and old" (ll. 233–34). Lippo's repeated avowal, "I'm a beast, I know" (l. 270), is an acknowledgment, not only of his sensual behavior, but also and primarily of his sensual art. His friendly setting of "things straight now, hip to haunch" (l. 44), is an attempt to relieve himself of the burden of tradition and the threat of "Brother Angelico" and "Brother Lorenzo" (ll. 235, 236). But this is terribly difficult, for the sanctioned aesthetic is personally intimidating. Lippo has absorbed his Prior's instructions to "forget there's such a thing as flesh / . . . paint the souls of men" (ll. 182–183) and must come to terms not simply with the official guardians of taste, but with his own self-monitoring doubts. He boasts that Medici patronage frees him of monastic supervision, "I'm my own master, paint now as I please— / Having a friend, you see, in the Corner-house!" (ll. 226–27), but it is clear that he is not unreservedly committed to following his own artistic bent. The monk argues with vigor and apparent conviction for an art that comprehends "the value and significance of flesh" (l. 268), but for all his eloquence about "the garden and God there / A-making man's wife" (ll. 266–67), Lippo is not free of the old standard. It has become incorporated into his artistic sensibility: "the old schooling sticks, the old grave eyes / Are peeping o'er my shoulder as I work" (ll. 231–32). The wisdom of tradition articulated by living authority figures has become internalized; and the result, as James Richardson writes, is that Lippo "is *not* his own master because he is still in rebellion against his own fears."[24] Lippo is polarized by the struggle between a spectral, but truly cogent, Prior-within and an authentic, original Beast.

An examination of Lippo's subselves shows that the antagonism between the flesh-denying, nay-saying defender of souls and the flesh-affirming defender of "the shapes of things" (l. 284) is founded on two conflicting notions of the self and two irreconcilable theories of vision. The Beast in Lippo knows that the soul acquires knowledge through the senses. There is nothing to fear in the expense of passion for the "soul and sense of him grow sharp alike" (l. 124). By rioting in the external, the soul or self discovers the non-temporal meaning of things. If the apprehending self hoards its energies and becomes disengaged from reality, then it misses truth. For most men the world is opaque; for them as for the Bishop of St. Praxed's, its beauty is impenetrably meaningless. The truth can be obtained only through engagement and the lending out of consciousness. Such participation is a form of love, and such love is a form of knowledge:

> What's it all about?
> To be passed over, despised? or dwelt upon,
> Wondered at? oh, this last of course!—you say.
> But why not do as well as say,—paint these

> Just as they are, careless what comes of it?
> God's works—paint anyone, and count it crime
> To let a truth slip.　　　　　　　　　(ll. 290–96).

Like Browning's lovers, Lippo understands that space and time can be collapsed. And, like the speaker of "Old Pictures in Florence," he knows that to pay attention to the visible, "to paint man man, whatever the issue!" (l. 148), is the best way "to bring the invisible full into play!" (l. 151). As celebrant of empirical reality, "this fair town's face, yonder river's line / The mountain round it and the sky above" (ll. 287–88), the artist becomes a high priest of the transcendent:

> 　　　　　We're made so that we love
> First when we see them painted, things we have passed
> Perhaps a hundred times nor cared to see;
> And so they are better, painted—better to us,
> Which is the same thing. Art was given for that;
> God uses us to help each other so,
> Lending our minds out. Have you noticed, now,
> Your cullion's hanging face? A bit of chalk,
> And trust me but you should, though! How much more,
> If I drew higher things with the same truth!
> That were to take the Prior's pulpit-place
> Interpret God to all of you!　　　　　(ll. 300–311).

Lippo's insight concerns not only the texture of reality but a truth about the nature of reality itself. The "things" of this world are wonderful; the universe is neither a blank nor an allegory, but a living mystery. This recognition, independent of any didactic content, is the motive of sensuous art.

The Prior-within knows something very different. He has no confidence in the relation between empirical truth and vision; "Faces, arms, legs and bodies like the true / As much as pea and pea! it's devil's-game!" (ll. 177–78). Lippo's rendition of his superior reveals the carmelite's hypocrisy and critical ineptitude, and it is tempting to interpret Lippo's mimicry as a form of dismissal.[25] But quite the opposite is true. Satire can be a form of resistance; and in this case, the vehemence of the monk's caricature suggests the cogency of the threat. Lippo feels intimidated by the traditional aesthetic. His interior Prior assumes that phenomena are mere distractions, non-essentials that impede vision:

Give us no more of body than shows soul!
. . . .
Why put all thoughts of praise out of our head
With wonder at lines, colours, and what not?
Paint the soul never mind the legs and arms!   (ll. 188–93).

He supposes, too, that wholeness of vision comes with distance, and he has Giotto and Fra Angelico on his side. He thinks that passion and sensory engagement are forms of dissipation; only by hoarding and imprisoning is truth achicvable. He would, in other words, stifle the emotions that attach to the world. Having no trust in the artist's negative capability, he believes that self-denial is the means to truth. Here lies the crux of Lippo's problem: aesthetic detachment is not just retreat; it is a form of self-effacement. The denial of the world necessarily means the suppression of the self that negotiates with the world. The Prior and the Beast are thus at odds, not simply over the data of the universe, or the flesh, but over the deployment of the soul's capabilities. It is not a matter of canvases only, but of Lippo's inner being.

It is in the light of this troubling subdivision that Lippo's self-accusations must be interpreted. He confesses his sensuality because he would like to be on easier terms with himself. He authenticates all that is fleshly in his life and art. He does not repress, blunt, or misdirect his guilt. And yet the twice-repeated charge, "I'm a beast, I know" (ll. 80, 270), lacks a certain energy. It seems pallid when compared with the abstract avowal by Pauline's poet that he is "knit round / As with a charm by sin and lust and pride" (ll. 846–7). To conclude, however, that Lippo's remarks are waggishly half-hearted is to miss the point. His self-flagellating is the result of self-division. The Prior-within is aggressively reproachful; he fragments the identity and prevents the artist from unhesitatingly acknowledging his "spirit's true endowments" ("Cristina" l. 20). Lippo's monologue is a self-appeasement exercise that does not work. Confession does not soothe his inner censor; self-derogation cannot liberate the artist's denied self or enable Lippo to paint God's works "just as they are, *careless* what comes of it" (l. 294, italics mine).

When he feels his distress most acutely, Lippo, like others before him, imagines external relief. Longing for official approval of his new style, he resents the discrepancy between what men say about renunciation and what they, in fact, believe about the value of the world; and he wants the issue "settled for ever one way" (l. 260). He even demands an answer of the Captain:

> you've seen the world
> —The beauty and the wonder and the power,
> The shapes of things, their colours, lights and shades,
> Changes, surprises,—and God made it all!
> —For what? Do you feel thankful, ay or no,
> For this fair town's face, yonder river's line,
> The mountain round it and the sky above,
> Much more the figures of man, woman, child,
> These are the frame to? What's it all about?   (ll. 282–90).

The style of the passage should be noted, for its energy is as revealing as what Lippo actually says. The monk engages his auditor, pummelling him with assertions—"You've seen the world"—and attacking him with questions—"For what?" "Ay or no," "What's it all about?" The vigorous stacking of phrases gives abstractions such as "colours, lights and shades" the quality of emotionally apprehended details, while the deft placement of a weak syllable before a medial caesura permits a metrical leap to the exulting conclusion, "and God made it all!" In the urgency of his appreciation, Lippo offers a second list of beauties. With a painterly sweep from foreground to background to sky above and a plunge back down to the human figures, he repeats his performance with a weak syllable and a medial caesura to spring another emphatic half line, "What's it all about?" Lippo's speech is as restless as his mood. Such significant adaptations are Browning's forte, and a brief look at a passage from "Andrea del Sarto" demonstrates how carefully Browning tailors his blank verse. Andrea's thoughts on Florence are very different from Lippo's:

> There's the bell clinking from the chapel-top;
> That length of convent-wall across the way
> Holds the trees safer, huddled more inside;
> The last monk leaves the garden; days decrease,
> And autumn grows, autumn in everything.   (ll. 41–45).

Andrea's style is meditative. Although he speaks aloud, his lines take no notice of Lucrezia, and the reader responds as if the passage were lyric rather than dramatic. In contrast to Lippo's visual range, Andrea's focus is fixed on the enclosed and huddled trees nearby. The difference in texture between his lines and Lippo's is also striking. Andrea's smoothness—he has one completely regular line whereas Lippo has none in a passage twice the length—his densely musical alliteration, and the nearly Tennysonian repetition of "autumn" express his elegiac mood. Andrea is chastened. Such passages reveal by their very sound the temperamental idiosyncrasies that are Browning's concern.

Lippo's resentment sometimes escalates to rage, for he has a strong suspicion that official sanction of his style will come only in time to bless the next generation of painters; "It makes me mad to see what men shall do / And we in our graves!" (ll. 312–13). If this is a frustrating intuition, it is also sustaining. It prevents Lippo from becoming another Andrea by precluding the fraudulent peace that capitulation to doubt would bring. Some issues cannot be "settled"; and despite Browning's preference for momentously unambiguous commitments, he considers an alternative: sustained tension, definition, not by unique choice, but by dialectic. This constitutes the originality of "Fra Lippo Lippi." Elsewhere in his poetry, Browning allows his monologists to engage in potentially illuminating scrutiny. Lippo, however, knows from the start the form his revelation should take and is denied the release he needs. Browning does not allow him to achieve confidence by a single act of will. In the monk's case, anxiety and turbulence are the means of lifelong self-realization. Aesthetic decision is a repeatable event in an ongoing struggle; commitment is an occasional achievement but a constant possibility. Lippo lives on the brink; every painting is a declaration.

A life of chronic consequence is difficult, and the boisterous Lippo is subject to the alternating tyranny of the Prior's doubts and the Beast's rages;

> I swallow my rage,
> Clench my teeth, suck my lips in tight, and paint
> To please them—sometimes do and sometimes don't.
> (ll. 242–44).

This zig-zagging, so painful to Lippo, is, however, precisely that which makes his art possible. His rage is a form of energy; it is not consuming, but propelling. Wreaking violence upon the "curtain and counterpane and coverlet" (l. 62), he escapes his room with a cry of "flesh and blood, / That's all I'm made of" (ll. 60–61) and plunges into the world of sense and passion. Fatigue sends him back to the studio until confinement and his next capitulation send him out into the world again. By a process of psychic pressure and counter-pressure, the self-denying force of Lippo's guilt precipitates his riotous self-assertion. The Censor's role is thus unexpectedly creative; the greater the tyranny, the more urgent the rebellion.

This sense of the positive relation between oppression and volatility, between inhibition and expression, informs the entire poem, particularly the account of Lippo's first sketches on the Carmelites' walls; "Thank you! my head being crammed, the walls a blank, / Never was such prompt disemburdening" (ll. 143–44). Lippo's explosion of figures and faces, "the black and white, / I drew them, fat and lean" (ll. 145–46), has the authority of all Browning's cataclysms; Lippo's artistic energy is like the rage of Saul that works "in the rock, helps it labour and lets the gold go" (l. 94). His drawings are truthful because his head has been "crammed"; a build-up of pressure has preceded them. The density and requisite compression of visual forms are the result of Lippo's childhood in the streets. For eight years the boy spent his time "watching folk's faces" (l. 114) to know who would help or hinder him in his thieving attempt at survival. The denied child learned to recognize the external signs of a man's personality and to penetrate his soul. Browning's concern is not with sociology or realistic detail, but with the relation between deprivation and sympathetic power. The boy's suffering intensifies his response to reality. Because of his need, the world becomes transparent and meaningful; familiar appearances serve as indices of things unseen. Deprivation, in other words, is a stimulant, and this seems to be true in the aesthetic as well as the psychological realm. The denied artist is driven to self-assertion.

Even the Medici household becomes important in the context of this dialectic. That Lippo's escapade should climax three weeks of virtual house arrest suggests that the palace is significant, not solely as a haven, but as a place to escape from, a point of departure. Physical enclosure is the dramatic counterpart of Lippo's more serious intangible confinement. The external forces that constrict him as child, man and artist correspond to the interior self-denying aspects of his being. Browning's point is that while such a condition is ordinarily stifling, in this instance it is creative. Hunger makes Lippo a participant in the lives of others; confinement causes him to join the revelers; the abstraction of the orthodox aesthetic drives him to an abundantly concrete art. Even Lippo's guilt is functional; it is the energy that generates his rage. If Lippo is unable to escape his interior oppressor, if his division cannot be apocalyptically healed in a momentous rush of definitive self-assessment, he can, nevertheless, live a dialectic of apocalyptic intensity.

Lippo will return to his patron and his patron's saint. And if, in guilt, he finishes the Jerome "knocking at his poor old breast / With his great round stone to subdue the flesh" (ll. 73–74), he will also, and with a far more complex mixture of feelings, paint a heavenly scene for Sant' Ambrogio's Church (l. 346). His angels will have a sensuous appeal that can be described only in a densely synesthetic manner. The "bowery flowery angel-brood" (l. 349) will have

> Lilies and vestments and white faces, sweet
> As puff on puff of grated orris-root
> When ladies crowd to Church at midsummer.   (ll. 350–52).

This painting is to include a self-portrait that will serve as more than a traditionally stylized signature. Lippo envisions this next work as the last scene of an imaginary drama. He sees himself emerging "out of a corner" (l. 361) knowing he is unfit to enter among "this pure company" (l. 368). The manner in which he is disposed of reflects his longing for authoritative sanction. The approval he cannot elicit on earth is offered by Saint Lucy; she reaches out her "soft palm" (l. 371) and speaks a "good word" (l. 386) on his behalf. This stylistically innovative painting has a double purpose, however, and is, as Roma King suggests, "a symbol of Lippo's whole experience."[26] Although it will dramatize Lippo's longed-for vindication, it will also serve to "make amends" (l. 343) for his behavior and wild talk to the guards. Lippo's monologue thus ends with the contradiction of wish fulfillment and simultaneous repentance. But there is "a pretty picture gained" (l. 389), a triumphantly sensuous picture born of this night's rebellion.

5

"Certainly I am not I"

From *Pauline* to *The Ring and the Book*, Browning's poetry assumes that self-consciousness is evidence of an absolute core of being. Whatever their difficulties coming to terms with themselves, his characters share the conviction that their existence is organized from within. They often, like Pauline's poet, express their ontological certainty in metaphors of center, core, and depth; Paracelsus speaks, for example, of an "inmost centre in us all" (1. 728) and the dying St. John of retreating into his soul; "So is myself withdrawn into my depths" (1. 76). The origin of being and the end of becoming, this interior self also serves as a standard by which Browning's characters judge their actions. The belief that it has been betrayed underlies general indictments such as "I lost myself" (*Pauline*, 1. 345) and uneasy rationalizations about some particular "chance, so lost" ("Andrea del Sarto" 1. 200). The hope of recovering these losses is the chief motive of Browning's speakers; their monologues, including those that are fraudulent and self-deceptive, are attempts, however imperfect, to sound the depths of self:

> Oh, how I wish some cold wise man
> Would dig beneath the surface which you scrape,
> Deal with the depths, pronounce on my desert
> Groundedly!　　　　　(*The Ring and the Book*, XI. 946–49)

The Prince of Hohenstiel-Schwangau and the Don who strolls in Pornic appear at first glance to fit predictably among Browning's introspective characters and to reinforce their belief in a subsistent self. Hohenstiel-Schwangau's intention of offering full "revealment" (1. 22) seems to affirm the object of other monologists' confessional scrutiny, while his boisterous self-confidence accords with their assumptions about authentic identity:

> Such is the reason why I acquiesced
> In doing what seemed best for me to do.
> . . . .
> Namely, that just the creature I was bound
> To be, I should become, nor thwart at all
> God's purpose in creation.   (ll. 231–32, 246–48).

The Don, like Caponsacchi, undertakes to expose his interiority; moved by the sight of a fluttering pennon, he launches his speculations with the question,

> do you know, there beats
> Something within my breast, as sensitive?—repeats
> The fever of the flag?   (ll. 43–45).

And he, too, alleges a bedrock confidence in his being:

> Now, there is one prime point (hear and be edified!)
> One truth more true for me than any truth beside—
> To-wit, that I am I.   (ll. 1063–65).

But early impressions of these characters are deceiving, for they exhibit, upon further acquaintance, personalities that defy metaphors of depth or center. Unlike Browning's earlier characters, they have no truth *au fond* that admits of revelation; they cannot expose what the Don, using a memorable image of dew encased in crystal, calls "the soul's self—/ . . . the centre-drop" (ll. 1789–90).[1] Their psychological kinsman is not the self-possessed John or even the evasive Andrea, but the erratic hero of *Red Cotton Night-Cap Country*. In the soliloquy preceding the leap that kills him, Leonce Miranda invokes the theory that human actions are intelligibly significant:

Along with every act—and speech is act—
There go, a multitude impalpable
To ordinary human faculty,
The thoughts which give the act significance,
Who is poet needs must apprehend
Alike both speech and thoughts which prompt to speak.

(ll. 3277–82).

Yet so unreconciled are the promptings of Miranda's nature that his life discredits his generalization; his deeds and thoughts can be apprehended, but neither the narrator nor the reader can perform the synthesis that might disclose an underlying character. Not only does the "true" Miranda remain undiscovered, his story is a "critique," as Walter Kendrick points out, of "methods of interpretation which regard surfaces merely as access to depths."[2]

The phenomenon of shallowness or the missing residuum of self is not wholly unprecedented in Browning's poetry, but the degree of emphasis is new and best understood as a further elaboration of his theory of elusiveness. The problem, as he conceives it in these works, is one of unresolved multiplicity. Instead of again considering those who honestly confess or unconsciously deceive themselves, Browning here turns his attention to the possibility that a man may fail not to discover but fail to *have* a unified, knowable identity. Each of these three—Hohenstiel-Schwangau, the Don, and Miranda—is capable of strong emotion but not of unswerving dedication; each is victim, in Miranda's phrase, of at least a double "fascination" (l. 3305) and is irremediably inconstant. Their disloyalty to others, moreover, is the result of a psychic chaos that precludes fidelity to a genuine self. One consequence of their multiplicity especially fascinating to Browning is the way it complicates the reader's sense of their honesty. When speaking of themselves, both the Prince and the Don can be caught in flagrant contradiction; and each stands justly accused of offering "tantalizing help / First to this, then the opposite," of "blowing hot and cold" as if afflicted by some "disease of the perception or the will" (*PH–S.* ll. 799–803). Neither explains himself consistently and the reader cannot confidently sort out the misrepresentations. Opposing statements have a way of sounding equally genuine. The Prince and the Don, like other of Browning's characters, are able casuists, but the difficulty assessing the sincerity of their remarks derives less from their argumentative skill than from their manner. Unembarrassed by contradiction, they allege conflicting motives with ease and apparent candor. Their remarkable facility cannot be attributed to some basic, though faultily expressed, unity of purpose; they possess, rather, a confessional ability to give virtually independent voice to fragments of their identities. They are the self-expressive descendants of Proteus. In this regard, both the Prince and the Don differ appreciably from the speakers of the confessions and the confessions manqués. Too disintegrated to feel self-betrayal, they exhibit none of the painful emotions—none of the shame, fear, and defensiveness—that Browning so often uses to guide the reader's intuition concerning a character's truest self. These monologues, despite their length, leave the impression of psychological anonymity.

Modern readers tend to share Swinburne's trenchant assessment that Browning "never thinks but at full speed" and are willing to unravel the thought of the poems;[3] Hohenstiel-Schwangau's theory of conservatism, the Don's "abstruser themes" (1. 1523), as well as the historical parallels with Napoleon III have each been carefully pursued.[4] Thanks in part to such efforts the poems themselves are no longer considered obscure; their portraiture, however, is still often dismissed as inadvertently ambiguous; "One obvious failing is [the poem's] lack . . . of a progressive revelation of the true character of the speaker;"[5] "The portrait is perhaps a failure . . . because the impression lacks intensity;"[6] "The personality . . . is no sooner created than it disintegrates."[7] While such comments indicate fairly the elusiveness of the characters, they err in quietly supposing that Browning falls short of his intention or means to offer hard-edged portraits. There is ample reason to think he does not. A satisfying way to approach the late poetry is to assume that the indeterminacy of the speakers is deliberate, not the consequence of Browning's running casuistically "amuck," but the poetry's origin and donnée.[8] Browning's comment to Isa Blagden concerning Napoleon III could serve, with only minor revisions, as an epigraph to *Hohenstiel-Schwangau* or *Fifine*: "I thought badly of him at the beginning of his career, *et pour cause*; better afterward, on the strength of promises he made, and gave indications of intending to redeem,—I think him very weak in the last miserable year."[9] Browning creates Hohenstiel-Schwangau and the Don because it pleases him to imagine the private assessment—

"what excuses he was likely to make for himself"[10]—of characters who elicit deservedly mixed reactions. He accepts as cause what readers sometimes misinterpret as effect and proceeds to explore the variable self-awareness of unsynthesized personalities.

To accommodate the chief opportunist of the era, Browning creates a new complication in the dramatic monologue. Hohenstiel-Schwangau's "ghostly" confession (1. 2092) seems to be conducted in Leicester Square for the benefit of a female companion; only at the end of the poem does the reader learn that the supposed exile is alone in his Residenz. Those who comment on this reversal ascribe the trick to something more than Browning's perversity, and Philip Drew's observation that the Prince "occupies the same relation to [the poem] as the poet himself" is particularly helpful.[11] By calling attention to Hohenstiel-Schwangau's role as the creator of his autobiographical scenario, Drew raises the issue of confessional license. Since the Prince's listener is an unobjecting figment of his imagination, he is at liberty to exhibit his psyche in any way he pleases. Not surprisingly, he chooses to construct a myth of coherent selfhood. Citing his "particular faculty" (1. 273) of conservatism, he boasts an instinctive single motive for all his actions:

> I like to use the thing I find,
> Rather than strive at unfound novelty:
> I make the best of the old, nor try for new.
> Such will to act, such choice of action's way,
> Constitute— . . .
> . . . —my own
> Particular faculty of serving God,
> Instinct for putting power to exercise.   (ll. 266–274).

The only pressure the Prince feels in the course of his reverie is inherent in his "real" situation, and in this respect his relation to the monologue differs from Browning's. The Prince inhabits the world of the poem and is, in fact, deliberating an action that will affect its history. The poem records his method of taking counsel. Since examination of the past generally clarifies one's principles and a look into the future helps discover consequences, Browning imagines his Prince doing both. He proceeds with a skill that moves Swinburne to praise Hohenstiel-Schwangau's intellect at the expense of his Napoleonic model:

> We may doubt . . . whether the perception of good or evil would actually be so acute in the mind of the supposed reasoner; whether . . . a veritable saviour of society . . . would in effect see so clearly and so far, with whatever perversion or distortion of view, into the recesses of the pit of hell wherein he lives and moves and has his being; recognising with quick and delicate apprehension what points of vantage he must strive to gain, what outposts of self-defense he may hope to guard, in the explanation and vindication of the motive forces of his nature and the latent mainspring of his deeds. This fineness of intellect and dramatic sympathy which is ever on the watch to anticipate and answer the unspoken imputations and prepossessions of his hearer, the very movements of his mind, the very action of his instincts, is perhaps a quality hardly compatible with a nature we might rather suppose, judging from public evidence and historic indication, to be sluggish and short-sighted.[12]

But for all his quickness in apprehending "points of vantage," the Prince finishes his meditation without accomplishing his purpose. His constructed myth of social "sustainment" (l. 710) is not cogent enough to direct his next action and he is unable to make the choice at hand. Hohenstiel-Schwangau's final indecisiveness—"Double or quits! The letter goes! Or stays!" (l. 2155)—is not the point of the poem so much as a dramatic symbol; Browning allows this slippery political figure to ponder his deeds without reaching a well-founded conclusion. The implication is that the series of episodes which make his life are similarly baseless; his career is *not* the result of "Character in Action."

The dramatic situation of *Fifine at the Fair* has an analogous ending with much the same import. An unfaithful husband currently interested in Fifine, the Don begins his monologue as an apologist for infidelity. But after lengthy speculation—some of the "most metaphysical and boldest," Browning boasted, "since *Sordello*"[13]—and the recollection of a brilliant dream, the Don reaches a penitent conclusion: "Inconstancy means raw, 't is faith alone means ripe / I' the soul" (ll. 2283-84). Henceforth he will be a "good-companion of the guild / And mystery of marriage" (II. 2320-21). But the Don, like his predecessor, is not yet ready to make a choice. Despite the usual association of subtlety and depth, of philosophical resolve and strength of character, the Don is capable of only partial sincerity and therefore hollow promises. Hardly is his chaste declaration made when he abruptly cancels it by hastening off to Fifine. Browning is less concerned with the

Don's tryst—though he clearly disapproves—than with the irresolute personality it symptomizes. The Don, like the Prince, is constitutionally incapable of steadfast personal commitment.

Part of Browning's point in these poems is that erratic characters don't necessarily perceive themselves as such. Despite the evidence of their waverings and betrayals, they believe in their own stability. The Prince, for example, knows others regard him as dishonorably unpredictable, but insists, like Miranda, on the principled intelligibility of his life. His explanation of his particular role invokes the traditional notion of coherent and unique individuality; "Each [man] has his own mind and no other's mode" (1. 182), his "path appointed him" (1. 215), and his "task imposed" (1. 648). For his own part, the Prince shares Paracelsus' certainty that his path is divinely illumined—"Just so / I have His bidding to perform" (ll. 156–57)—and speaks repeatedly of following his "true ordinance" (1. 203) and "rule of life" (1. 253). His illusory sense of personal direction is statistically measurable, for, as Clyde de L. Ryals notes, "the word 'law' occurs with greater frequency in *Prince Hohenstiel-Schwangau* than in any other of Browning's poems."[14] The Prince is also sure of the meaning of disobedience; those who transgress their being's law are moral hypocrites, "Our insincerity on both our heads!" (1. 217). But protestations about sincerity and ordained individuality do not endow the Prince with these qualities, nor do similar remarks transform his successor in *Fifine*. The Don knows he is accused of inconstancy but attempts exoneration with a sophisticated theory of self. The Don pursues women to alleviate his sense of personal unreality, or, as he says, to "convince unreasonable me / That I am, anyhow, a Truth, though all else seem / And be not" (ll. 1357–59). Marital infidelity is, in his view, virtually imperative, a form of fidelity to the self. What may appear to his wife as a lack of integrity is, for him, an existential necessity. Readers from 1873 to the present have found the Don's argument persuasive, and while some have been shocked at Browning's apparent defense of adultery, others have praised his Don's anti-bourgeois courage. Both reactions need modification, however, for Browning values elements of the Don's metaphysics more than his conduct and arranges matters so that the vagrant husband himself provides the theory that distinguishes philandering from legitimate ways of affirming one's reality. But before one ventures into the ironies of *Fifine*, a look at the simpler cross-purposes of *Prince Hohenstiel-Schwangau* is in order.

As with earlier monologues, Browning manages Hohenstiel-Schwangau's poem so that its shape and language suggest the personal qualities its argument denies. Browning knows that a man is revealed by the form of his creations and writes for his Prince a conspicuously subdivided reverie. Hohenstiel-Schwangau begins discussing his life in the first person, but shifts his method halfway into the poem and allows a composite historian to describe, in third person, "what [the Prince] never was, but might have been" (l. 1224). In this pseudo-biography, Thiers-Hugo praises an allegorical Head of State for eschewing the opportunism counselled by "Sagacity." The reader soon realizes, as Roma King says, "that Thiers-Hugo is merely one aspect of the multiple Prince, his long-submerged idealistic youth, and that Sagacity is another, his disillusioned maturity"; this discovery leads inevitably to the question whether "behind the diverse manifestations of Prince Hohenstiel" there really is a "single man."[15] But the reader doesn't have to wait to meet Sagacity to have such doubts. Long before the poem's divided structure becomes apparent, there are indications of the Prince's indeterminacy.

At the very outset, Hohenstiel-Schwangau's preparatory, throat-clearing remarks suggest the mentality of a sphinx. When he compares his auditress' desire to know him with that of European statesmen who "have sometimes wished the same, / . . . and had their trouble for their pains" (ll. 4–5), his extreme delight in baffling others becomes apparent. He regards personal mysteriousness as a "good trick" (l. 12), and although he now promises to dispense with it and "make the matter plain" (l. 25), the reader suspects that Hohenstiel-Schwangau may be the enigma he imitates. He professes to know the solution to his own riddle, but there is reason to doubt his self-perception. It seems likely that the Prince has never reconciled the extremes of his personality. His favorite metaphor of the "plaguey quadrature" (l. 59) seems a clue to his interior state, for while it argues that knowledge of the "whole man" is as impossible as a squared circle, it also indicates how easily the Prince can dismiss incongruities with a cliché. Like so many of Browning's speakers, he can glamorize his weakness and consider himself one of the "abstruser problems" of "moral mathematics" (ll. 50, 52). He displays, moreover, no fear that his being is unformed, deficient, or chaotic, only a smug pleasure in what he supposes to be a nature more enigmatic than most.

Convinced that he is a primally coherent individual, "a being by myself" (1. 122), he argues without a trace of conscious doubt (but with a great deal of dramatic irony) for the continuity of the self amid flux. His acceptance of the theory of evolution lifts him to the heights of self-assertion. When "modern Science" declares,

> that mass man sprung from was a jelly-lump
> Once on a time; he kept an after course
> Through fish and insect, reptile, bird and beast,
> Till he attained to be an ape at last
> Or last but one, (ll. 987–91),

the Prince responds with pleasure:

> God takes time.
> I like the thought He should have lodged me once
> I' the hole, the cave, the hut, the tenement,
> The mansion and the palace; made me learn
> The feel o' the first, before I found myself
> Loftier i' the last, not more emancipate;
> From first to last of lodging, I was I,
> And not at all the place that harboured me. (ll. 1011–18).

"I was I"; Browning is having great fun with his oblivious Prince and arranges a stunning reversal of this phrase. Towards the end of the Thiers-Hugo biography, the question of royal illegitimacy happens to arise—"there's nothing so unproveable / As who is who, what son of what a sire" (ll. 2056–57)—when the clock suddenly chimes. Startled from his reverie, Hohenstiel-Schwangau blurts out; " 'Who's who?' was aptly asked, / Since certainly I am not I!" (ll. 2078–79). He means literally that the referent of the word "I" has shifted. The subject of the biography is not the "I" of the Leicester Square "revealment" nor the "I" who is roused to consciousness in the Residenz. But Hohenstiel-Schwangau's shockingly terse "I am not I" invites wider application. The referent of the "I" is indeed shifty. Since Hohenstiel-Schwangau could at any time be any number of possible selves, his use of the first person in necessarily unreliable. His subjectivity is so variable that the meaning of his pronoun changes with the circumstances and alters with each utterance. The "I" does not correspond to an integrated self.

Browning's interest in the possibility that "I am not I" is the thematic link between *Prince Hohenstiel-Schwangau* and *Fifine at the Fair*, but with a major difference in handling. The personal discrepancies the Prince ignores are openly confronted by the Don. He admits his longing for law and lawlessness, for Elvire and Fifine, and sees his inconstancy mirrored by the instability of institutions and the impermanence of nature. Watching how the nightfall changes the landscape, he turns to Elvire with the question:

>   Are you unterrified?
> All false, all fleeting too! And nowhere things abide,
> And everywhere we strain that things should stay.
>
> (ll. 1468–70).

Perhaps all is illusion since, quite obviously, all is "falsehood, fleetingness" and change (l. 1472). Certainly, the Don argues, one's chief aim in life is the task of eliciting a "self-vindicating flash" (l. 352) and of proving that oneself, at least, is real:

>   Alack, our life is lent,
> From first to last, the whole, for this experiment
> Of proving what I say—that we ourselves are true!
>
> (ll. 1396–98).

Despite the clarity of this insight, the Don's monologue as a whole indicates that his personal "experiment" is unsuccessful. The poem argues, like its predecessor, that the individual who is inconstant—and not simply disloyal to his wife or allies, though these are symptomatic infidelities—may be radically untrue. False and changeable, both the Don and the Prince may be said to lack being; their identities are illusions created by the "I" pronoun. One may conclude, making due allowance for their existence as Browning's creations, that the poet regards his Prince and Don as unreal characters.

This conclusion may be expressed in a variety of ways. Some would argue that these travesties of the confessional mode indicate Browning's growing skepticism about man's prospects for self-knowledge and the authentic use of subjective utterance.[16] Others would urge, more strongly, that Browning questions not only the possibility of self-revelation but even the existence of the self. In *Victorian*

Revolutionaries, for example, Morse Peckham argues for the pervasiveness of such an attitude, not only in *Hohenstiel-Schwangau* and *Fifine*, but throughout the dramatic monologues:

> They are, in Oscar Wilde's famous phrase, truly sphinxes without secrets, for the secret of the Browning dramatic monologues is that there is no secret. Behind the speaker is everything and nothing.[17]

Readers are as unlikely to agree on the extent of Browning's skepticism as they are on his optimism or pessimism. Nor is disagreement a reason for dismay provided one realizes its cause. The wide divergence of opinion concerning Browning's thought is the result of a tendency he recognizes and comments on. He writes in *Fifine* of the possibility of explaining "the glories by the shames / Mixed up in man" (ll. 1874–75). The phrase is a good description of Browning's habit of thinking in polarities:

> For at what moment did I so advance
> Near to knowledge as when frustrate of escape from ignorance?
> Did not beauty prove most precious when its opposite obtained
> Rule, and truth seem more than ever potent because falsehood
> reigned?   (*La Saisiaz* ll. 361–64).

Instinctively Browning imagines the truth that lodges in a false context, the possibility that goes unrealized, the triumph that comes through failure, the failure that is a resisted success. Thus the skepticism he expresses is always relative and contingent. That he sometimes imagines characters who lack a "deepest sentient self" (*La Saisiaz* l. 398) does not argue his complete disbelief, but a daring willingness to consider the "shame" that is missed "glory." The Prince and the Don take their place among Browning's many characters, not as a cynical comment on their revelations and gropings toward integrity, but as extreme figures in a continuum. The one end is peopled by converts who discover their truest selves; then come the resisters who elude their epiphanies and live with a sense of lost chances; and then follow the Prince, the Don, and Miranda who vacillate faithlessly among possible selves.

   This continuum, it should be noted, is thematic and not chronological, for even in his late career Browning is concerned with its full range. The Protean natures of the Prince and the Don may seem, in their poems, to reduce sincerity to a nearly irrelevant concept, but Browning does not abandon it. These two confessions may leave their speakers as erratic as ever, but their failures do not wholly undermine Browning's trust in subjective scrutiny. Browning can still affirm, as in *La Saisiaz*, the integrity of the self and the value of introspection. The speaker, who in this poem represents Browning himself, expresses many of the same opinions as his predecessors. He is as willing as the Don to question the reality of others: "If my fellows are or are not . . . mere surmise" (ll. 263–64). And while he is sure of his existence—"I am, can recognize / What to me is pain and pleasure: this is sure" (ll. 261–62)—he is not at all clear what this certitude means—"I myself am what I know not" (l. 260). He is also a man divided, so shocked by Miss Smith's sudden death as to debate the "controverted doctrine" (l. 210) of personal immortality using the double voices of Fancy and Reason. Unlike his predecessors, however, the speaker gives the impression of depth and resolution. When he promises to listen for the truth "whispered by my soul to me" (l. 150), one believes in both his soul and his genuine attention to its promptings. It hardly matters whether his argument is compelling; the poem succeeds as an expression of subjectivity and convinces the reader of the speaker's sincerity. Jerome McGann puts the matter cogently when arguing "The Case of Browning":

> Reading the poem, we are led to take the ideas seriously because we must take the speaker seriously. In the end we need not agree with a single opinion put forward by Browning's dramatized self, but we cannot regard those opinions with indifference or contempt. Everything in the poem reinforces the crucial image of Browning as a thoughtful, sensitive and very flexible man, who has not arrived at his conclusion hastily. We grant him, in other words, the truth of his convictions (hardly more): at least this is what the poem intends us to do.[18]

Miss Smith's elegist is not the only one allowed the "truth of his convictions" in Browning's later work. A poet of Croisic, René Gentil-homme, is allowed a moment of illumination that he communicates with spontaneous directness: "Brimful of truth, truth's outburst will convince / (Style or no style) who bears truth's brunt" (ll. 303–04). But the pre-eminent "escape / Of soul" ("Two Poets of Croisic" ll. 346–7) validated in Browning's late years is that of Christopher Smart. This parleying is of special interest for it affirms both Smart's vision and his expression. He achieved, in Browning's opinion, a perfect relation of subject, word, and object: "Smart . . . pierced the screen / 'Twixt thing and word, lit language straight from soul" (ll. 113–14). He managed to express subjective and "real vision" in objective and "right language" (l. 152). That Smart's triumph occurred only once moves and saddens Browning, but its singularity does not diminish its value. The uniqueness of the achievement may even be enhancing; such is the case with Guercino's "The Guardian Angel":

> And since he did not work thus earnestly
> > At all times, and else has endured some wrong—
> I took one thought his picture struck from me,
> > And spread it out, translating it to song.   (ll. 50–53).

Browning, at any rate, compares the "Song to David" to an extraordinarily splendid chapel in an otherwise quietly tasteful house and, using his favorite metaphor of theophany, likens Smart's perception to a transfiguration that wraps the poet in flame (ll. 76–86) and an apocalyptic view of "the old things thus made new" (l. 148). Such insight and verbal completion are as rare and yet as verified as Caponsacchi's apocalypse of self. Since Christopher Smart is Browning's only hero between Milton and Keats, the reaction to his song is as grateful as to the *Old Yellow Book*. Each is proof that "the miracle" does happen and that truth finds vent in lives and words.

The parleying with Smart should be kept in mind as one listens to the Don's and the Prince's complaints about language:

> > Words struggle with the weight
> So feebly of the False, thick element between
> Our soul, the True, and Truth!   (*Fifine* ll. 943–45).

> Ah, if one had no need to use the tongue!
> How obvious and how easy 't is to talk
> Inside the soul.   (*PH-S.* ll. 2090–92).

If the service of words disappoints these characters, the failure is attributable only in part to the limitations of the medium. The more important cause is the faultiness of their personalities and the fraudulence of the linguistic assistance they desire. Each would like to be verbally incarnated as something he is not and to reify in confession a wholeness foreign to his being. Their objection to language is that it does not misrepresent them well enough, or, in the economy of Browning's irony, that it reveals too much. Given their intentions, however, it follows that their complaints are justified; their language, even at the level of syntactic organization, belies their avowed meanings. Hohenstiel-Schwangau, for example, likes to speak of himself as one driven by a mandated sense of purpose, and yet he constantly generates sentences that lose their momentum. Grammatically suspended to the point of stalemate, they cast doubt on the strength of his motivation and anticipate his final need to resort to dice. While trying, at one point, to explain his support of the *status quo*, the "Saviour of Society" employs a familiar form of hypothetical argument; "even if A, then B." Since readers are accustomed to such syntax, they assume that the Prince will reach a conclusion *in spite of A*; upon reading his thesis about "destruction," they correctly anticipate the repudiation that comes in the final clause. The recognizable pattern provides forward or horizontal momentum; and although the sentence is elaborately suspended, readers know how to deal with the intermediate material. Imaginatively, if not orally, subordination is acknowledged by lowering the voice and proceeding a bit more quickly. But knowing is not the same as executing, and the inordinate length of the qualifying material and the proliferation of clauses within clauses require too many successive drops of pitch and impossible increases of speed.

> Why, even prove that, by some miracle,
> Destruction were the proper work to choose,
> And that a torch best remedies what's wrong
> I' the temple, whence the long procession wound
> Of powers and beauties, earth's achievements all,
> The human strength that strove and overthrew,—
> The human love that, weak itself, crowned strength,—
> The instinct crying "God is whence I came!"—
> The reason laying down the law "And such
> His will i' the world must be!"—the leap and shout
> Of genius "For I hold His very thoughts,
> The meaning of the mind of him!"—nay, more,
> The ingenuities, each active force

That turning in a circle on itself
Looks neither up nor down but keeps the spot,
Mere creature-like, and, for religion, works,
Works only and works ever, makes and shapes
And changes, still wrings more of good from less,
Still stamps some bad out, where was worst before,
So leaves the handiwork, the act and deed,
Were it but house and land and wealth, to show
Here was a creature perfect in the kind—
Whether as bee, beaver, or behemoth,
What's the importance? he has done his work
For the work's sake, worked well, earned a creature's praise;—
I say, concede that same fane, whence deploys
Age after age, all this humanity,
Diverse but ever dear, out of the dark
Behind the altar into the broad day
By the portal—enter, and concede there mocks
Each lover of free motion and much space
A perplexed length of apse and aisle and nave,—
Pillared roof and carved screen, and what care I?—
Which irk the movement and impede the march,—
Nay, possibly, bring flat upon his nose
At some odd break-neck angle, by some freak
Of old-world artistry, that personage
Who, could he but have kept his skirts from grief
And catching at the hooks and crooks about,
Had stepped out on the daylight of our time
Plainly the man of the age,—still, still, I bar
Excessive conflagration in the case.   (ll. 655–95).

Inevitably the reader fails to keep pace with the sentence; the sense of
the ending wanes as momentum dissipates. Length is not the only rea-
son the reader must slow down; the qualifying material is vividly pic-
torial (the hero of the age falls on his nose), lively with metaphor
(genius leaps and shouts in the procession from society's temple),
packed with alliterations, quotations and active verbs. The intervening
lines exert a vertical force and refuse to stay subordinated; they ob-
trude on the reader's attention and assert the primacy of their meaning.
The result is that vertical cancels horizontal and the propelling force of
Hohenstiel-Schwangau's conservative meaning is dispelled. The
Prince seems to sense this for he gives his theme a boost about halfway

through ("I say, concede," l. 679), but the damage is irrevocable. The ineffectively end-directed syntax exposes its weakly oriented speaker.

The dubious subordination of clauses within sentences is matched by a similar relation between large blocks of Hohenstiel-Schwangau's argument. To cite one instance, the Prince's explanation of his conservator's "style and title" (l. 294) is initially emphatic while its reiteration in successive sentences keeps his argument moving. The reader is not confused, therefore, when the man who claims to be "preserving you . . . the old, / Nor aiming at a new and greater thing" (ll. 315–16) begins describing the rejected role of social innovator. The Prince's enthusiasm, however, amounts almost to affirmation; the length and vividness of the subordinate passage distracts attention almost completely from Hohenstiel-Schwangau's conclusion. The argument is too long to quote in full, but the interruption can be cited. For thirty lines Browning lends Hohenstiel-Schwangau the use of a favorite theme and obviously enjoys his descriptions of sudden transformations:

> A breath of God made manifest in flesh
> Subjects the world to change, from time to time,
> Alters the whole condition of our race
> Abruptly, not by unperceived degrees
> Nor play of elements already there,
> But quite new leaven, leavening the lump,
> And liker, so, the natural process. See!
> Where winter reigned for ages—by a turn
> I' the time, some star-change, (ask geologists)
> The ice-tracts split, clash, splinter and disperse,
> And there's an end of immobility,
> Silence, and all that tinted pageant, base
> To pinnacle, one flush from fairyland
> Dead-asleep and deserted somewhere,—see!—
> As a fresh sun, wave, spring and joy outburst.
> Or else the earth it is, time starts from trance,
> Her mountains tremble into fire, her plains
> Heave blinded by confusion: what result?
> New teeming growth, surprises of strange life
> Impossible before, a world broke up
> And re-made, order gained by law destroyed.
> Not otherwise, in our society
> Follow like portents, all as absolute

Regenerations: they have birth at rare
Uncertain unexpected intervals
O' the world, by ministry impossible
Before and after fulness of the days:
Some dervish desert-spectre, swordsman, saint,
Law-giver, lyrist,—oh, we know the names!
Quite other these than I.   (ll. 323–52)

Although Hohenstiel-Schwangau reaffirms his own position in the final half-line, he has invested counterbalancing energies in both sides of his argument. Intellectually he may reach his preferred conclusion, but the reader cannot dismiss the evidence of fondness for the opposition. Hohenstiel-Schwangau may claim God's warrant to be a conservator, but he imagines the re-creator as a divinely incarnated being ("a breath of God made manifest in flesh") arriving in the apocalyptic "fulness of days." And since the Prince formerly held radical views—"as he helps, I helped once" (l. 1065)—this passage makes clear that his zeal hasn't completely burned out. Far from being committed to his present role, the Prince might, given the proper circumstances or cast of the dice, appropriate that of his alter-ego. Instead of a sense of Hohenstiel-Schwangau's purposefulness, the reader carries away from this passage an impression of the Prince's chameleon nature. No sooner does he present a case, then he becomes caught up by it. Hence the partial truth of his objections about language; his words don't create the impression he intends. His inability, however, to subordinate clauses and arguments is related to his lack of personal coherence. Hohenstiel-Schwangau's nature is such that he wants to lose nothing, but keep all; "all capabilities—/Nay, you may style them chances if you choose—/ All chances then" (ll. 504–06).

A similar conclusion can be reached about the Don who tries, in his own way, to maintain all his "chances." As Elvire's husband but Fifine's visitor, he attempts the life of a "God-fearing householder" (l. 134) as well as a gypsy "losel" (l. 139). For this he is accused of finding "no value fixed in things" (l. 496) and of coveting "all you see, hear, dream of" (l. 497). In this restless openness to possibilities, the Prince and the Don recall the heroes of Browning's first narratives. Pauline's poet is so amorphously enthusiastic as to express the wish to "be all, have, see, know, taste, feel all" (l. 278); Aprile is tormented by his "yearnings to possess at once the full / Enjoyment" of his infinite love

(*Paracelsus* II. 388–89): and Sordello feels himself "equal to being all" (I. 548). In the early poems, Browning's heroes are proud of their un-channeled longing, but cognizant also of its dangers; Pauline's poet best expresses their collective discovery with the comment that "a mind like this must dissipate itself" (1. 291). If Hohenstiel-Schwangau is un-aware of his dissipation and pays ignorant lip service to his being's fancied "law," his successor is more perceptive. Fifine's admirer, like Pauline's poet, advances a theory of focus:

> each soul lives, longs and works
> For itself, by itself,—because a lodestar lurks,
> An other than itself,—in whatsoe'er the niche
> Of mightiest heaven it hide.   (ll. 900–02).

But to know one needs a lodestar is not to be drawn by it, and in prac-tice the Don pursues many "an other" in a way that is frankly and reductively sexual. This is not to imply that Browning's personal mores or his guilt over an infidelity to the memory of Elizabeth accounts solely for the morality of the poem.[19] The Don's method of discovering himself through women is problematic to Browning because, like Sor-dello during his years at Goito, the philandering husband fails to prize the objects of his attention. Both the minstrel and the Don overesti-mate their contribution to the dialectic of the self and other:

> . . . in the seeing soul, *all* worth lies, I assert,—
> And *nought* i' the world, which, save for soul that sees, inert
> Was, is, and would be ever,—stuff for transmuting,—null
> And void until man's breath evoke the beautiful.
>   (ll. 824–27, italics mine).

Each in his egotism reduces the world to a series of merely personal opportunities. The Don, however, is more aggressive and blunt than Sordello. A suddenly noted detail in the scene is appropriated for his argument: "dolphins, my instance just!" (1. 1290). An unfinished sculp-ture is equally self-serving; the possession of an Eidothee by Michel-angelo redounds to the credit of the "special soul" who sees what others miss (1. 873). Even Elvire's plainness offers gratifying possibilities. After caricaturing her face in a sand sketch, the Don instructs her to trust that he alone perceives her hidden beauty: "See yourself in my soul!" (1. 808). The women he finds outwardly attractive, the Mimis, Toinettes, and Fifines, have only the significance of auxiliaries to his vanity (Section 71). The merest female notice seems to him existential tribute, and his efforts to realize himself through these women pass easily over into narcissism:

> Women rush into you, and there remain absorbed,
> . . . any sort of woman may bestow
> Her atom on the star. . . .
> Women grow you.   (ll. 1173–79).

Eager and willing to collect such female atoms, the Don praises women's powers of "absolute self-sacrifice" (1. 731) and has absolutely no comprehension of *their* individual autonomy. He is utterly incapable of the awe expressed in "One Word More" or of Caponsacchi's chaste surrender.

The irony of the Don's psychic imperialism is that he seems, during the climactic retelling of his carnival dream, to understand what is necessary for a valid relation between the self and the "other than itself" (1. 901). His first view of the crowd in St. Mark's square fills him with disgust. Viewed from a lofty vantage point, they seem morally grotesque:

> Age reduced to simple greed and guile,
> Worn apathetic else as some smooth slab, erewhile
> A clear-cut man-at-arms i' the pavement, till foot's tread
> Effaced the sculpture, left the stone you saw instead,—
> Was not that terrible beyond the mere uncouth?
> Well, and perhaps the next revolting you was Youth,
> Stark ignorance and crude conceit, half smirk, half stare
> On that frank fool-face, gay beneath its head of hair
> Which covers nothing.   (ll. 1703–11).

This attitude of revulsion is the opposite side of his readiness to appropriate what pleases him. His response to those outside himself—whether to a Fifine or a masquer—is contaminated by his assumed superiority and his instinctive rejection of all autonomy but his own. Whether approving or censorious he remains, in his arrogance, a perceiver quite remote from the object of perception. In the dream, however, this distance is collapsed. As the Don descends into the crowd, "a groundling like the rest" (l. 1738), they become less repellent. The dreamer finds, having "looked / The nearlier" that the revelers are less deviant than he supposed and that his initial revulsion is replaced by a more humane sentiment:

> here, I found brutality encroach
> Less on the human, lie the lightlier as I looked
> The nearlier on these faces that seemed but now so crook'd
> And clawed away from God's prime purpose. They diverged
> A little from the type, but somehow rather urged
> To pity than disgust.   (ll. 1542–47).

This transformation teaches the Don that the viewer of the human spectacle "must nor fret / Nor fume, on altitudes of self-sufficiency" (ll. 1881–82). The proper response is not moral judgment but acceptance: "bid a frank farewell to what—we think—should be, / And, with as good a grace, welcome what is—we find" (ll. 1883–84). The Don learns too that genuine familiarity does more than dispel contempt; it breeds enlightenment:

> whereby came discovery there was just
> Enough and not too much of hate, love, greed and lust,
> Could one discerningly but hold the balance, shift
> The weight from scale to scale, do justice to the drift
> Of nature, and explain the glories by the shames
> Mixed up in man, one stuff miscalled by different names
> According to what stage i' the process turned his rough,
> Even as I gazed, to smooth—only get close enough!
> —What was all this except the lesson of a life?
>   (ll. 1870–78).

If the rhetorical question in the final line has a triumphant ring, it is *not* because the Don has corroborated its "lesson" in his life. The authority of the line derives from Browning himself. Both in content and in method, the carnival "discovery" dramatizes Browning's aesthetic achievement. The Don's approach to the "mimes / And mummers" (ll. 1869–70) is a good analogy for Browning's repeated descent from the "altitudes of self-sufficiency." The Venetian dream is Browning's own version of Robert Langbaum's well-known analysis of how the tension between sympathy and judgment enables Browning to achieve his end, "the end being to establish the reader's sympathetic relation to the poem, to give him 'facts from within.' "[20] The dramatic method is Browning's strategy for getting "close enough."

The success of this technique is evident in the poems it produces. "Childe Roland," "Andrea del Sarto," "Fra Lippo Lippi" and others are permanent achievements, but one detects a non-aesthetic advantage as well. Browning gains through his adventures in the interiority of his characters the knowledge his Don only spuriously claims:

> Just so I glut
> My hunger both to be and know the thing I am,
> By contrast with the thing I am not.   (ll. 1815–16).

Browning, in other words, defines himself in opposition to what is outside himself. Indulging in a legitimate form of promiscuity, he engages with many "an other" and thereby comes to terms with his own identity. Browning's practice differs from that of his solipsists in the same way the grounded dreamer of the carnival differs from the pursuer of Fifine. Browning's relation to the world is not imperialistic; he does not absorb or disesteem it. On the contrary, the complex particularity of his many characters indicates how compelling he finds their demands. He is respectful of their individuality and immensely reassured by their autonomy. In this quality of mind he resembles Gerard Manley Hopkins who records in his journal that "what you look hard at seems to look hard at you."[21] Both poets find it existentially verifying to pay the tribute of invested energy to the world outside themselves. In this sense any of Browning's poems that "look hard at" their characters may be said to be autobiographical. Even those that give no evidence of Browning's opinions, no scrap of direct biographical information, are valuable embodiments of his confrontations with the other; through them he brings himself into being. Patricia Ball summarizes this view of Browning very cogently. She finds his pursuit of "dramatic challenges" to be egotistical "not in the sense of a man using all his creations as mouthpieces" but rather as the expression of an

> urge to self-discovery which drives him ceaselessly out of himself, making him a continual explorer of possibility, at a level deeper than that of the 'philosophizing' so frequently attributed to him. He speaks not out of what he knows, but in order to realize the experiencing self. . . .[22]

Browning's Don, however, continues his narcissistic adventures and fails where his creator ordinarily succeeds. He remains as untrue as before his dream and as unreal as Hohenstiel-Schwangau; his discourse is neither more nor less unified than the Prince's reverie. It maintains conflicting points of view, defends opposite modes of action, and gives no hint that the speaker is seriously worried by his vacillations. The Don, like the Prince, is very much at ease. Both, in fact, are so verbally flowing that their volubility becomes counter-effective. The reader worries, on occasion, that it is all too easy and that the speakers are not investing much in their arguments. At such times there is an almost irresistible temptation to skim long passages waiting for some indication that the speaker is troubled and earnest. Such skimming, of course, has unfortunate aesthetic consequences; when it starts, the psychological process described in the carnival sequence comes to a halt. Sensing the speaker's absence from the argument, the reader refuses to descend from the heights or to become sympathetic.

Bishop Blougram provides a helpful contrast in this regard. Despite the indirection and length of his apology—it approaches half that of *Hohenstiel-Schwangau* though it seems considerably shorter—Blougram holds the reader's interest in a way the Prince and Don do not. One reason for this is his commitment to Gigadibs' supposed premises. It is dramatically immaterial whether they are valid bases for Christian apology; Blougram wants to be understood on these terms and not others. They have been deliberately chosen and though he shifts them carefully, he does not abandon them. His investment in what he assumes to be a winning strategy makes his "Apology" more engaging than the later poems. Another way of explaining the difference between the impact of Blougram's discourse and that of the Don or the Prince is to consider the strength of the Bishop's desire to humiliate Gigadibs. Browning has looked hard at people like Blougram and can therefore allow the prelate to assert himself forcefully. But in the later works Browning has less respect for his characters' autonomy; this is partly because they are less autonomous, but partly because Browning's interests are changing. He cares more about the play of ideas and somewhat less about his speakers. He pays them less attention and presses them, a trifle imperialistically, into discursive service. The result is that the reader sometimes feels talked at but not looked "hard" at.

* * * *

Throughout his poetry Browning attempts, however unique his characters or unusual their crises, to propel them towards an authentic "consciousness / Of self" (*Pauline* ll. 268–69). If a particular individual fails in this enterprise, it is not because his creator feels uncertain how the self may be known; on the contrary, Browning has favorite intuitions on the subject. He conceives of passions as reflexive. His lovers and artists who reach generously out are also reaching in, and their acts of surrender are liberating. Their method of immersion in the other may also be applied to the past. Since "old events" (*Paracelsus* V. 509) bristle with meaning, genuine remembrance can be epiphanic. But not every man is capable of surrender or honesty. For some, the true self remains undisclosed because its exposure threatens self-esteem. Keenly aware of man's tendency to protect a cherished image, Browning permits his characters to work hard at avoiding themselves. Aware, too, that some individuals are irresolvably diffuse, he allows them to expose their multiplicity.

Browning's genius is that he understands cowardice. He knows that the bullying of fact or phenomena is the result of unconscious fear and that surrender can be an act of trust. Those who dread negating their identities, like Andrea or the Bishop of St. Praxed's, remain ignorant of the universe and of themselves. Those who fear commitment, like the philandering Don, are unable to value the autonomy that would verify their own: the autonomy of the other. Though many of Browning's characters deceive themselves, and though their manipulations often leave them unenlightened, Browning does not patronize them. Instead he wonders at the variety of their exertions; they use candor as a defense and ingeniously misremember the past. Fascinated by their subtle forms of guile, Browning can regret, but he cannot wholly despise, their egotism.

His intelligence about their ways of sustaining self-estrangement informs his notion of conversion. To be saved, in the secular as in the religious sense, is to become truly discerning. Whether epiphany is a unique or repeated event, it is a matter of self-possession. The potential convert may, like Saul, have forsaken a life he should lead, or like Gigadibs, be pursuing a role he should abandon. In either case, conversion allows the emergence of the authentic self. Such triumphs are costly, however, and their consequences sobering. Even young Duchesses will have to go "where the haters meet / In the crowded city's horrible street / Or . . . alone thro' the morass" ("Flight of the

Duchess" ll. 661–63). If the victorious Roland is not annihilated, he must, when he lowers his slug–horn, use more projections to cross another wilderness, because there is always a wilderness, and projections, even when their limits as strategies are known, are the only way to make passage. The artist born ahead of his time and the new man reborn into a corrupt old world will often find cause for rage; and those who endure the "initiatory spasm" need both the reassurance given by the gypsy crone:

> Trial after trial past,
> Wilt thou fall at the very last
>
> . . . .
>
> With the thrill of the great deliverance.
>   ("Flight of the Duchess" ll. 608–11).

and the more somber encouragement of the Pope; "Be unhappy, but bear life" (*Ring and the Book* X. 1212).

Notes

1. *"In the Confessing Vein"* pages 1–36.

1. William C. DeVane, *A Browning Handbook* 2d ed. (New York: Appleton, 1955), p. 47; Oswald Doughty and John Robert Wahl, eds., *Letters of Dante Gabriel Rossetti*. I (Oxford: Clarendon Press, 1965), 32 33.
2. Quotations are from Sir Frederic George Kenyon's edition of the *Works*, 10 vols. (London, 1912), cited hereafter as *Works*.
3. DeVane, p. 62.
4. *Natural Supernaturalism: Tradition and Revolution in Romantic Literature* (New York: Norton, 1971); *The Confessional Imagination: A Reading of Wordsworth's Prelude* (Baltimore: Johns Hopkins Univ. Press, 1974).
5. W. David Shaw offers a helpful outline of the characteristics of confession in his chapter "The Autobiography of a Mourner: *In Memoriam*" in *Tennyson's Style* (Ithaca: Cornell Univ. Press, 1976); for a historical treatment of autobiography, see Roy Pascal's *Design and Truth in Autobiography*. (London: Routledge, 1960).
6. From the sermon "On God's Vineyard" in *John Wesley*, ed. Albert C. Outler (New York: Oxford Univ. Press, 1964), p. 108. The edition is cited hereafter as *Wesley*.
7. Roma A. King, Jr., *The Focusing Artifice* (Athens: Ohio Univ. Press, 1968), p. 49, believes that Pippa's auditors are saved; W. David Shaw, *The Dialectical Temper: The Rhetorical Art of Robert Browning* (Ithaca: Cornell Univ. Press, 1968), pp. 45 63, argues compellingly that Pippa's "songs are a formal rather than efficient cause of each of the conversions" in the poem. For a vehemently different view cf. D. C. Wilkinson, "The Need for Disbelief: A Comment on *Pippa Passes*," *Univ. of Toronto Quarterly*, 29 (1960), 137–151.
8. Richard Curle, ed., *Robert Browning and Julia Wedgwood: A Broken Friendship as Revealed by Their Letters* (New York: Stokes, 1937), p. 15.
9. Wesley wrote in his *Journal*, "The faith I want is 'a sure trust and confidence in God, that, through the merits of Christ, my sins are forgiven and I reconciled to the favor of God.' " His definition is from "Of the True and Lively Faith" in IV, *Certain Sermons or Homilies, Appointed to Be Read in Churches . . .* (Oxford, 1684) and is orthodox. *Wesley*, p. 49.
10. *Wesley*, pp. 51–69.

11. "Preface" to "Alastor," *Shelley: Poetical Works*, ed. Thomas Hutchinson and G. M. Matthews (London: Oxford Univ. Press, 1970), p. 15; for an extended comparison of "Alastor" and *Pauline*, see Park Honan, *Browning's Characters: A Study in Poetic Technique* (New Haven: Yale Univ. Press, 1961), pp. 11–17.

12. *Browning's Youth* (Cambridge: Harvard Univ. Press, 1977), p. 200, 235.

13. Maynard, p. 235.

14. Maynard, p. 58; the quotation is from Elisha Coles, *A Practical Discourse of God's Sovereignty: With Other Material on Points Deriving Thence* (London, 1673), p. 102, a source cited later as Coles.

15. Maynard, p. 58.

16. Frederic George Kenyon, *Robert Browning and Alfred Domett* (London: Smith, Elder, 1906), p. 141.

17. Jerome H. Buckley, *The Victorian Temper: A Study in Literary Culture* (New York: Random/Vintage, 1964), p. 88.

18. *Autobiography of John Stuart Mill*, ed. John Jacob Coss (New York: Columbia Univ. Press, 1924), p. 94. Cited hereafter as Mill.

19. Mill, pp. 94, 95.

20. Thomas Carlyle, *Sartor Resartus*, ed. Charles F. Harrold (New York: Odyssey, 1937), p. 162.

21. Carlyle, p. 163.

22. *The Poetry of Experience: The Dramatic Monologue in Modern Literary Tradition* (New York: Norton, 1957), p. 15.

23. Mill, p. 94.

24. Buckley, p. 92.

25. *Confessions*, trans. Vernon J. Bourke (New York: Fathers of the Church, Inc., 1953).

26. Abrams, pp. 36–37.

27. Abrams, p. 48.

28. *Wesley*, pp. 51–53.

29. *Wesley*, pp. 53–54.

30. *Wesley*, p. 54.

31. *Wesley*, p. 55.

32. *Wesley*, p. 66.

33. *Wesley*, p. 61, n. 11.

34. "Lines Composed a Few Miles Above Tintern Abbey," *The Poetical Works of William Wordsworth*, ed. E. DeSelincourt (Oxford: Oxford Univ. Press, 1940), II. 261.

35. *In Memoriam*, section I, *The Poems of Tennyson*, ed. Christopher Ricks (London: Longman, 1969), p. 865.

36. Wordsworth, II. 261.

37. *In Memoriam*, section XCV, p. 946.

38. Carlyle, p. 168.

39. Mill, p. 99.

40. Coles, p. 155.

41. Arthur Symons remarks in *An Introduction to the Study of Browning* (London:

Dent, 1906) that Browning's "best landscapes are as brief as they are brilliant" p. 24; for an irreverent, but perceptive, response to Browning's suddenly changing settings see C. S. Calverly's parody "The Cock and the Bull" cited by Honan p. 209.

> . . .Ut,
> Instance, Sol ruit, down flops sun, et and,
> Montes umbrantur, out flounce mountains.

42. Elvan Kintner, ed., *The Letters of Robert Browning and Elizabeth Barrett Barrett 1845–1846*, 2 vols. (Cambridge: Harvard Univ. Press, 1969), I. 404.
43. Wordsworth, II. 400–01.
44. *The Poems of Samuel Taylor Coleridge*, ed. Ernest Hartly Coleridge (London: Oxford Univ. Press, 1912), p. 365.
45. *The Letters of John Keats 1814–1821*, ed. Hyder E. Rollins (Cambridge, Harvard Univ. Press, 1958) I, 238–39.
46. Shelley, p. 602.
47. See Patricia Ball's chapter "Sincerity: A Victorian Criterion" in *The Central Self: A Study in Romantic and Victorian Imagination* (London: Althone Press, 1968), pp. 152–65, for a discussion of Wordsworth's 1802 Preface, Romantic conceptions of sincerity, and the way "these are debased after 1830 into expectations that poets shall be piously sincere."
48. *Letters*, I. 54.
49. *Letters*, I. 143.
50. *Letters*, I. 544.
51. *Letters*, I. 174.
52. "Overwrought passions and emotions" are among the characteristics Donald Hair cites in his discussion of Browning and the Spasmodics; *Browning's Experiments with Genre* (Toronto: Univ. of Toronto Press, 1972), p. 4.
53. Cited by Richard D. Altick, "Browning and the Spasmodics," *Studies in Browning and His Circle*, 2 (1974), 58.
54. William S. Peterson and Fred L. Stanley, "The J. S. Mill Marginalia in Robert Browning's *Pauline*: A History and Transcription," *Papers of the Bibliographical Society of America*, 66 (1972), 135–170.
55. Maynard, p. 213.
56. *Rousseau: Oeuvres Complètes*, ed. Michel Launay (Paris: Editions du Seuil, 1967) I. 121.
57. Rousseau, I. 226, 124.
58. Rousseau, I. 122.
59. Rousseau, I. 135.
60. Rousseau, I. 162.
61. Lionel Trilling, *Sincerity and Authenticity* (Cambridge: Harvard Univ. Press, 1971), p. 58.
62. For a discussion of the sources and incongruities of the Bishop's Biblical epigrams see Charles T. Phipps, S.J., "The Bishop as Bishop: Clerical Motif and Meaning in 'The Bishop Orders his Tomb at St. Praxed's Church," *Victorian Poetry*, 8 (1970), 199–208.

63. *Letters*, I. 53–54.
64. Keats, I. 387.
65. *Works*, I. 178.
66. William C. DeVane and Kenneth L. Knickerbocker, eds., *New Letters of Robert Browning* (New Haven: Yale Univ. Press, 1950), p. 18.
67. "Essay on Shelley" in *The Poetical Works of Robert Browning*, ed. George Robert Stange (Boston: Houghton Mifflin, 1974), p. 1009.

2. *"In Thunder From the Stars":* *Rescue and Renewal* pages 37–68.

1. Shelley, pp. 577–79.
2. William C. DeVane, "The Virgin and the Dragon," in *Robert Browning: A Collection of Critical Essays*, ed. Philip Drew (London: Methuen, 1966), pp. 98, 99.
3. That Browning planned but never wrote a "resuscitation-scene" indicates how satisfying—perhaps unconsciously so—he found the intense expectation of the present ending, for he certainly was capable of returning to a poem and finishing it as much as a decade later. See the discussion of "Saul" in this chapter and Curle, p. 86, for the reference to "Artemis Prologizes."
4. The phrase is from William Cadbury's "Lyric and Anti-lyric Forms: A Method for Judging Browning," in *Browning's Mind and Art*, ed. Clarence Tracy (New York: Barnes and Noble, 1970), p. 34. This collection will be cited hereafter as Tracy. For an equally favorable interpretation of the controversial Lady Gismond, see Ian Jack, *Browning's Major Poetry* (Oxford: Clarendon Press, 1973), pp. 86–88.
5. For Eliot's review see *Browning: The Critical Heritage*, ed. Boyd Litzinger and Donald Smalley (New York: Barnes and Noble, 1970), pp. 174–77. Many but by no means all readers share this assessment of Blougram. See F. E. L. Priestley's influential defense, "Blougram's Apologetics," *Univ. of Toronto Quarterly*, 15 (1945–46), 139–47, which argues that Blougram's "only approach to Gigadibs is through premises he will accept"; and Roma A. King Jr., *The Bow and the Lyre: The Art of Robert Browning* (Ann Arbor: Univ. of Michigan Press, 1964), pp. 76–99; and Shaw, *Dialectical Temper*, pp. 203–12. The latter believe, respectively, that Blougram "has in reserve a better defense of religion" (p. 99) and that he descends "from his religious plateau to argue as an unbeliever" (p. 204).
6. For a reference to Guido Reni, whose *St. Sebastian* is in the Dulwich College Picture Gallery, see *Letters*, I. 509.
7. DeVane, *Handbook*, pp. 40–41.
8. *Letters*, I. 135.
9. David Sonstroem, " 'Fine Speeches Like Gold' in Browning's 'The Glove,' " *Victorian Poetry*, 15 (1977), 8.
10. Robert G. Laird, " 'He Did Not Sit Five Minutes': The Conversion of Gigadibs," *Univ. of Toronto Quarterly*, 45 (1976), 295–313. Laird identifies Richard Henry (Hengist) Horne, Browning's friend who emigrated to Australia, as the original of Gigadibs; but see Ian Jack, p. 207, who points to Alfred Domett.

11. DeVane, p. 254.
12. F. E. L. Priestley, "Some Aspects of Browning's Irony," in Tracy p. 136; Shaw, p. 224.
13. For an extended discussion of the Biblical imagery of "Saul," see Ward Hellstrom, "Time and Type in Browning's 'Saul,' " *ELH*, 33 (1966), 370–89.
14. Mill, p. 94.
15. T. J. Collins, *The Poems of Matthew Arnold*, ed. Kenneth Allott (London: Longmans, 1965), p. 288.
16. *Robert Browning's Moral-Aesthetic Theory: 1833–1855*, (Lincoln, Univ. of Nebraska Press, 1967), p. 91.
17. Curle, pp. 54–55.
18. King, *Bow*, p. 121.
19. In "The Ongoing Testament in Browning's 'Saul,' " *Univ. of Toronto Quarterly*, 43 (1974), 151–68, Elizabeth Biemans reaches a similar conclusion by a different route; she calls attention to the "abstracted, yet fatherly touch of Saul's hand on David's head" and argues that "David, seeking in love to save Saul, discovers himself loved and saved, and Saul, for all his helplessness, has an important role in the process," p. 161.
20. James Joyce, *Stephen Hero*, new ed. J. J. Slocum and H. Cahoon (New York: New Directions, 1955) p. 211.
21. William O. Raymond, *The Infinite Moment and Other Essays in Robert Browning*, 2d ed. (Univ. of Toronto Press, 1965), pp. 19–20.
22. J. Hillis Miller, *The Disappearance of God: Five Nineteenth Century Writers* (New York: Schocken, 1965), p. 99.
23. Abrams, p. 47.
24. Langbaum, pp. 50–51.
25. King, *Focusing Artifice*; King emphasizes aspects of the poem other than those stressed here, but reaches the same conclusion, specifically, that whether actual or imaginative, the speaker's "moment of personal encounter proved apocalyptic" p. 88.
26. Quoted by Hoxie N. Fairchild, *Religious Trends in English Poetry* (New York: Columbia Univ. Press, 1957), IV. 145.
27. For a thorough discussion of Browning's sources, and his misreading of them, see Beatrice Corrigan, *Curious Annals: New Documents Relating to Browning's Roman Murder Story* (Univ. of Toronto Press, 1956).
28. A. K. Cook, *A Commentary upon Browning's The Ring and the Book* (1920; rpt. Hamden, Conn.: Archon, 1966), p. 125 and *The Old Yellow Book*, trans. Charles W. Hodell, 2d ed. (Carnegie Institution of Washington, 1908), LXXXIX, LXXV, trans. pp. 71–72, 74.
29. William S. Peterson, ed., *Browning's Trumpeter: The Correspondence of Robert Browning and Frederick J. Furnivall 1872–1889* (Washington, D.C.: Decatur House, 1979), p. 90.
30. Richard D. Altick and James F. Loucks, *Browning's Roman Murder Story: A Reading of The Ring and the Book* (Chicago: Univ. of Chicago Press, 1968), 184–225.

31. *The Alien Vision of Victorian Poetry: Sources of the Poetic Imagination in Tennyson, Browning, Arnold* (Princeton: Princeton Univ. Press, 1952), p. 131.
32. "A Note on the Conversion of Caponsacchi," *Victorian Poetry*, 9 (1968), 274.
33. For a similar evaluation of this episode, see Shaw, *Dialectical Temper*, p. 282; he argues that Pompilia's influence "makes the Church's asceticism a cogent demand."
34. As Sister Richard Boo observes in "The Ordeal of Giuseppe Caponsacchi," *Victorian Poetry*, 3 (1965), the stages of Caponsacchi's religious conversion can be traced in his attitude towards Rome. Though the city has always been his goal, "his motives have shifted appreciably" p. 182.

3. *"No Bar Stayed Me": The Confession Manqué*   pages 69–103.

1. *Findings* (New York: Atheneum, 1971), p. 40.
2. Cf. J. B. Bullens, "Browning's 'Pictor Ignotus' and Vasari's 'Life of Bartolommeo Di San Marco,' " *Review of English Studies*, N.S. 23 (1972), 313–19. If one accepts Bullens' identification of the unknown painter as Fra Bartolommeo, it becomes possible to argue on the basis of extra-poetic, historical evidence that the painter actually could have rivaled Raphael. The poem, however, suppresses this identification and supplies no evidence, factual or temperamental, of the painter's alleged talent.
3. *Letters*, I. 365.
4. James Joyce, "Araby," in *Dubliners*, ed. Robert Scholes and Richard Ellmann (New York: Viking Press, 1958), p. 35.
5. Honan, p. 190.
6. *Letters*, I. 500.
7. King, *Bow*, p. 64.
8. "A New (Old) Reading of 'Bishop Blougram's Apology': The Problem of the Dramatic Monologue," *Victorian Poetry*, 10 (1972), 248.
9. David Ewbank, "Bishop Blougram's Argument," *Victorian Poetry* 10 (1972), 257–63, also calls attention to this line and observes that "the Catholic, indeed the Christian position is, of course, that man's nature is fallen and that it *is* his business to remake himself," p. 263.
10. Honan, p. 232.
11. "Browning's 'Karshish' and St. Paul," *Modern Language Notes*, 72 (1957), 495.
12. King, *Focusing Artifice*, p. 111.
13. *Letters*, I. 457–8.
14. *Letters*, I. 467.
15. *Letters*, II. 756.
16. Raymond, p. 216.
17. Shaw, *Dialectical Temper*, p. 150.
18. *Letters*, I. 176.
19. *Letters*, II. 638.

20. See F. E. L. Priestley's hint in "Some Aspects of Browning's Irony." in Tracy, p. 131; and Wendell V. Harris, "Browning's Caliban, Plato's Cosmogony, and Bentham on Natural Religion," *Studies in Browning and His Circle* 3 (1975), 95-103.
21. Arthur O. Lovejoy, *The Great Chain of Being: A Study of the History of an Idea* (New York: Harper, 1960), p. 47.
22. For a discussion of the relation of the poem to the Psalm, see Barbara Melchiori, *Browning's Poetry of Reticence* (New York: Barnes and Noble, 1968), pp. 143-46.
23. Honan, p. 177.
24. Miller, p. 129.
25. The phrase is Donald Smalley's. See the introduction to his edition of *Browning's Essay on Chatterton* (Cambridge: Harvard Univ. Press, 1948), p. 76; see also Isobel Armstrong, "Browning's Mr. Sludge, 'The Medium,' " *Victorian Poetry*, 2 (1964), in which she analyzes "the strategy of the medium's defense" and concludes that "very little of the detail is gratuitous," p. 1.

4. *"When a Soul Declares Itself":
Varieties of Triumph* pages 105-137.

1. "Childe Roland and the Perversity of Mind," *Victorian Poetry*, 4 (1966), 253.
2 Curle, p. 7.
3. Kintgen, p. 253.
4. Lovejoy, p. 11.
5. For a lengthy discussion of the sources and interpretations of "Childe Roland," see Ian Jack, pp. 179-94.
6. The paradoxical quality of Roland's experience has, of course, received illuminating comment by others. William Cadbury, in Tracy, p. 40, writes that "the discovery of a lack of order is itself an ordering"; and Roma King, in *Focusing Artifice*, p. 91, observes that the "meaninglessness of the end . . . is apparent, a discovery that emphasizes the meaningfulness of the action itself."
7. Symons, p. 210.
8. DeVane, *Handbook*, pp. 295-98; Raymond, pp. 19-51.
9. See E. D. H. Johnson, "Romantic, Victorian, Edwardian," *The Princeton University Library Chronicle*, 38 (1977), 198-224, for a description of the Robert H. Taylor Collection, and Plate 41 for a reproduction of page 48 from Browning's copy of Shelley. I am grateful to Mr. Taylor for permitting me to examine this unique volume.
10. John D. Gordan, *Joint Lives: Elizabeth Barrett and Robert Browning: A Selection of Works from the Henry W. and Albert A. Berg Collection of English and American Literature* (New York: New York Public Library, 1975), p. 35.
11. See Virginia M. Hyde, "The Fallible Parchment: Structure in Robert Browning's 'A Death in the Desert,' " *Victorian Poetry*, 12 (1974), 125-36, for a discussion of the "discrepancies" in the poem whereby Browning "simulates some of the care-

fully plotted textual problems of a manuscript in the hands of a higher critic," p. 134; and Elinor Shaffer, "Browning's St. John: The Casuistry of the Higher Criticism," *Victorian Studies* 16 (1972), 205–21, for evidence that Browning follows Renan in making John confess his absence from the Cross.

12. DeVane notes that Browning changed 1. 51 of "By the Fire-side" from "hour's feat" to "moment's feat" in the 1863 version, p. 221.

13. *Works of Thomas Hardy*, Wessex Edition, (London: Macmillan, 1912) Vol. I, 301.

14. *Letters*, I. 3–4.

15. "Browning's Art and 'By the Fire-side,' " *Victorian Poetry* 15 (1977), 148–49.

16. *Letters*, I. 379.

17. Isobel Armstrong, "Browning and the 'Grotesque' Style," in *The Major Victorian Poets: Reconsiderations*, ed. Isobel Armstrong (Lincoln: Univ. of Nebraska Press, 1969), once objected to the "manner" of this stanza, pp. 107–8; but in a more recent article, "Browning and Victorian Poetry of Sexual Love," in *Writers and Their Background: Robert Browning*, ed. Isobel Armstrong, (Athens, Ohio Univ. Press, 1975), she withdraws the objection and writes that the passage "succeeds in miming rank, restless, rapidly growing sexual feeling which can find no direct expression and so becomes lewd and burdensome to itself," pp. 269–70.

18. *The Sense of an Ending: Studies in the Theory of Fiction* (London: Oxford Univ. Press, 1966), p. 4.

19. Shelley, pp. 529–31.

20. *Letters*, I. 74.

21. A failure to see that Caponsacchi's monologue is a confession, and not simply a narrative, led one contemporary reviewer to fault Caponsacchi's retrospective; "So passionate a man would surely have been more inclined to plunge in medias res," J. P. Mozley, *Macmillan's Magazine* 19 (April 1869), 548; cited by Ezzat Khattab, *The Critical Reception of Browning's The Ring and the Book: 1868–1889 and 1951–1968* (Salzburg: Institut Für Englische Sprache Und Literatur Univ. Salzburg, 1977), p. 49.

22. For the opposite view that Browning's "immediate object in 'Fra Lippo Lippi' was to defend the artist from social tyranny," cf. William Irvine, "Four Monologues in Browning's *Men and Women*," *Victorian Poetry* 2 (1963), 159.

23. For analyses of Lippo's strategies and emotions, see Honan, pp. 153–55; Armstrong, *Reconsiderations*, p. 118; King, *Bow*, pp. 32–33. See also Leonee Ormond, "Browning and Painting," in *Writers and their Background*, pp. 184–210; Ormond places "Fra Lippo Lippi" and "Andrea del Sarto" within "that popular Victorian genre, illustrating the lives of the old masters," p. 185, and accompanies the text with plates.

24. See James Richardson's discussion of "Fra Lippo Lippi" in the chapter "Other Lives: Hardy and Browning," in *Thomas Hardy: The Poetry of Necessity* (Chicago: Univ. of Chicago Press, 1977).

25. Shaw, for example, sees in Lippo "a comic philosopher who mimics the self-delusion of spiritual experts like the Prior in order to expose their contradictions," *Dialectical Temper*, p. 156.

26. King, *Bow*, p. 50.

5. *"Certainly I am not I"*   pages 139–162.

1. A favorite image of Browning's; see *Letters*, II. 933.
2. "Facts and Figures: Browning's *Red Cotton Night-Cap Country*," *Victorian Poetry*, 17 (1979), 343–363.
3. *Browning: The Critical Heritage*, p. 391.
4. Trevor Lloyd, "Browning and Politics," in *Writers and their Background*, pp. 142–67; Charlotte Crawford Watkins, "The 'Abstruser Themes' of Browning's *Fifine at the Fair*," *PMLA*, 74 (1959), 426–37; Leo A. Hetzler, "The Case of Prince Hohenstiel-Schwangau: Browning and Napoleon III," *Victorian Poetry* 15 (1977), 335–50.
5. Philip Drew, *The Poetry of Browning: A Critical Introduction* (London: Methuen, 1970), p. 302.
6. Honan, p. 237.
7. J. M. Cohen, *Robert Browning* (London: Longmans, 1952), p. 140.
8. Raymond, p. 310.
9. *Dearest Isa: Robert Browning's Letters to Isabella Blagden*, ed. Edward C. McAleer (Austin: Univ. of Texas Press, 1951), p. 371.
10. *Browning to His American Friends: Letters Between the Brownings, the Storys and James Russell Lowell*, ed. Gertrude Reese Hudson (Cambridge, England: Bowes, 1965), p. 167.
11. Drew, p. 298.
12. *Critical Heritage*, p. 392–93.
13. DeVane, p. 365.
14. *Browning's Later Poetry: 1871–1889* (Ithaca: Cornell Univ. Press, 1975), p. 54.
15. King, *Artifice*, p. 169.
16. King, *Artifice*, p. 166.
17. *Victorian Revolutionaries: Speculations on Some Heroes of a Culture Crisis* (New York: Braziller, 1970), pp. 117–18.
18. *Swinburne: An Experiment in Criticism* (Chicago: Univ. of Chicago Press, 1972), pp. 69–70.
19. For the connection between Browning's proposal to Lady Ashburton and his writing of *Fifine*, see Raymond, pp. 105–28; Ryals, pp. 60–61.
20. Langbaum, p. 78.
21. *The Journals and Papers of Gerard Manley Hopkins*, ed. Humphry House, completed by Graham Storey (London: Oxford Univ. Press, 1959), p. 204.
22. Ball, p. 213.

Index

173